JONAH, MICAH, NAHUM, HABAKKUK

by
John M Riddle

40 Beansburn, Kilmarnock, Scotland

ISBN-13: 978 1 914273 47 6

40 Beansburn, Kilmarnock, Scotland

www.ritchiechristianmedia.co.uk

Typeset by John Ritchie Ltd., Kilmarnock
Printed by Bell & Bain Ltd., Glasgow

Contents

Preface

In March 2017, John Ritchie Ltd kindly published notes covering Friday evening Bible Class discussions at Mill Lane Chapel, Cheshunt, on the books of Hosea, Joel, Amos and Obadiah.

In the goodness of God, and the further kindness of the Publishers, it has now become possible to give further consideration to the so-called 'Minor Prophets' (they were, of course, 'Major Men of God'), and the present volume covers the books of Jonah, Micah, Nahum and Habakkuk.

For the record, the discussions on Micah, took place between November 2004 and February 2005, and on Habakkuk in October 2004. Alas, the archivist did not record the dates relating to the studies in Jonah and Nahum, but it does not require 'rocket science' to guess that they were conducted during the latter part of 2004.

As here, dates may be forgotten, but we must never forget that in the Old Testament (and, for that matter, in the New Testament), "holy men of God spake as they were moved by the Holy Ghost" (2 Pet. 1:21). Time has not silenced the voice of God through His servants the prophets. The apostle Paul reminds us that "Whatsoever things were written aforetime were written for our learning, that we through patience and comfort (margin, 'encouragement') of the scriptures might have hope" (Rom.15:4).

Once again, it should be said that this volume, like its predecessors, does not purport to be a commentary in the usual sense of the word. No attempt is made to be exhaustive.

As before and, again, not as a mere courtesy, the Bible Class at Cheshunt remains genuinely indebted to John Ritchie Ltd for their willingness to publish its notes, something first mooted by Mr. John Grant, and to Mr. Fraser Munro and his colleagues for their invaluable help in editing the material submitted to them. The Bible Class also continues to be grateful to Miss Lesley Prentice for having checked and corrected the original manuscripts, something she continues to do, and to Mr. Eric Browning for his considerable help in continuing to send copies of current studies by Email to a wide readership.

The prayerful desire of the Mill Lane Bible Class is that, in the goodness of God, this volume will prove to be a channel of "edification, and exhortation, and comfort" (1 Cor. 14:3).

Finally, should you feel constrained to ask, 'And what about the rest of the Minor Prophets?', the answer lies in the somewhat hackneyed expression - 'Watch this space'. All, of course, God willing.

John Riddle
Cheshunt, Hertfordshire
October 2023.

JONAH

1) Introduction

Read 2 Kings 14:23-25; Jonah 1:1-3; Matthew 12:38-41

In beginning to study the book of Jonah, notice should be taken of the following: ***(1)*** Jonah and his colleagues; ***(2)*** Jonah and his preaching; ***(3)*** Jonah and his critics.

1) JONAH AND HIS COLLEAGUES

It is neither accurate nor complimentary to call them 'The Minor Prophets'. On the contrary, they were major men of God. At one time, these books circulated together, and were known as 'the Book of the Twelve'. They have been rather beautifully described as 'the twelve-jewelled crown of the Old Testament'.

Jeremiah tells us that the true prophet, "stood in the counsel of the LORD, and hath perceived and heard his word" (Jer. 23:18). He also tells us that on eleven occasions, God rose up early to speak to Israel through the prophets. See, for example, Chapter 7 verse 25, "Since the day that your fathers came forth out of the land of Egypt unto this day I have even sent unto you all my servants the prophets, ***daily*** rising up early and sending them". Their ministry spanned the centuries of Israel's history as follows, and it is rather significant to notice that God "left not himself without witness" (Acts 14:17).

1. $5^{th}/6^{th}$ Centuries B.C. Haggai, Zechariah, Malachi, Ezekiel, Daniel

2. 7th Century B.C. Nahum, Habakkuk, Zephaniah, Jeremiah, Obadiah

3. 8th Century B.C. Hosea, Amos, Micah, Isaiah

4. 9th Century B.C. **Jonah,** Joel.

5. 10th Century B.C. Elijah, Elisha.

Note: the above table is 'rough and ready' in the extreme. ***You*** could easily do some 'fine tuning'. Why not spend an evening or two on the subject, and then share your conclusions? Joel and Obadiah are not easily placed, but don't let that put you off! The table goes back beyond the era of the 'writing prophets' to the days of Elijah and Elisha. This is to demonstrate that God was never silent. You could incorporate other 'non-writing' prophets in the table.

2) JONAH AND HIS PREACHING

As you can see from the above, Jonah probably belonged to the ninth century B.C., and may well have preached during the reign of Jeroboam II. See 2 Kings 14 verse 25, "He restored the coast of Israel from the entering of Hamath unto the sea of the plain, according to the word of the LORD God of Israel, which he spake by the hand of his servant Jonah, the son of Amittai, the prophet, which was of Gath-hepher". While Jeroboam's reign commenced in B.C. 825, Jonah's prophecy could, of course, have been made before this date. However, we do learn that Jonah's preaching was more extensive than his one eight-word sermon recorded in Jonah 3 verse 4. We also learn that his preaching was not always as dark and foreboding as the message to Nineveh suggests. After all, if we only had the book of Jonah, his preaching would go down in history as the most miserable ever heard. It would also go down in history as the most successful!

While each of the 'Minor Prophets' (with renewed apologies to them) is quite distinctive, Jonah is particularly unique. The message of the book is the man himself. As we have noticed, Jonah's sermon at Nineveh must rank as the briefest in Scripture. You wouldn't even have time to take a sneaky look at your watch whilst he was preaching! But God has a great deal to teach us from the attitude and experience of Jonah personally.

3) JONAH AND HIS CRITICS

The events described in the book of Jonah are authenticated by the Lord Jesus: "For as Jonas was three days and three nights in the whale's belly; so shall the Son of man be three days and three nights in the heart of the earth. The men of Nineveh shall rise in judgment with this generation, and shall condemn it: because they repented at the preaching of Jonas; and, behold, a greater than Jonas is here" (Matt. 12:40-41). Despite this, the story of Jonah has been dismissed in the past for two reasons:

i) That no whale has a gullet big enough to permit the passage of a man's body.

ii) That no city answering to the size and description of Nineveh actually existed.

Both objections have been totally refuted by scientific discovery in the first case and by archeological evidence in the second. We will refer to this evidence at the appropriate time. But it is worth making the point now that we do not need scientific and archeological evidence before we can trust the Bible. Since it is the Word of God, it ***must*** be correct. People who doubt the accuracy of Scripture are really calling the Lord Jesus a liar, and that should settle the argument for every Christian.

This brings us to the first of three ways in which we can study the book of Jonah.

A) A GREATER THAN JONAH

The Lord Jesus said, "Behold, a greater than Jonas is here". Whilst Jonah was a type of Christ in his experience, he was certainly not a type of Christ personally. His character serves to emphasise the perfection of the Lord Jesus. Remember,

No mortal can with Thee compare
Among the sons of men:
Fairer art Thou than all the fair
That fill the heavenly train.

It is interesting to notice that Jonah's native town was Gath-hepher. This stood very near to the site of the later Nazareth. The Pharisees overlooked this fact in saying, "Search, and look: for out of Galilee ariseth no prophet" (John 7:52). "But Jonah, by his Galilean origin, as well as in other ways, foreshadowed the Greater than he, Who was also 'of Galilee'" (H.P. Barker, *Christ in the Minor Prophets*).

Each of the four chapters of the book emphasises at least one way in which the Lord Jesus is "greater than Jonah".

Chapter 1: Greater than Jonah in His obedience

"Jonah rose up to flee unto Tarshish from the presence of the LORD" (v.3). The Lord Jesus said, "I was not rebellious, neither turned away back" (Isaiah 50:5); "The works which the Father hath given me to finish, the same works that I do" (John 5:36). "He ... became obedient unto death, even the death of the cross" (Phil. 2:8). He said, "Lo, I come: in the volume of the book it is written of me, I delight to do thy will, O my God" (Psalm 40:6-7, quoted in Hebrews 10:7). As we shall see, Jonah's disobedience arose from fear of being discredited. (See Chapter 4 verses 1-2.) The Lord Jesus was completely aware of the way in which He would be discredited, but was in no way deterred from accomplishing His God-given work.

Chapter 1 reminds us of other ways in which the Lord Jesus was "greater than Jonah". Jonah had no power over the storm which threatened his life and the lives of the mariners. The Lord Jesus "arose, and rebuked the wind, and said unto the sea, Peace, be still. And the wind ceased, and there was a great calm" (Mark 4:39). The presence of Jonah brought fear to the mariners, but the presence of the Lord Jesus brought peace to the disciples. He said, "It is I; be not afraid" (John 6:20).

The mariners were saved from a watery grave by throwing Jonah overboard. Men "crucified the Lord of glory" (1 Cor. 2:8), but His death became the means of their salvation.

The mariners had to drag the truth out of Jonah: he made no attempt to volunteer information. But the Lord Jesus said, "I spake openly to the world" (John 18:20).

The message, "Go to Nineveh", involved a long and difficult journey, and meant preaching to a hostile and cruel audience. But think of the journey taken by the Lord Jesus, and think of the hostility and cruelty that He faced.

Chapter 2: Greater than Jonah in His experience

Don't underestimate Jonah's experience. It was quite horrible. He was under no misapprehension about the reason. When the mariners "took up Jonah, and cast him forth into the sea" (1:15), they were actually acting on God's behalf: "For ***thou*** hadst cast me into the deep, in the midst of the seas" (2:3). Compare Acts 2 verse 23, "Him, being delivered by the determinate counsel and foreknowledge of God, ye have taken, and by wicked hands have crucified and slain". The Lord Jesus suffered under divine judgment. In the words of H.P. Barker: "Delivered up to the Gentiles, He was by them buffetted, scourged and crucified. But into deeper depths yet He went. The waters came into His soul. He sank in 'the mire of depth' where there was no standing, into 'depths of waters' where the floods overflowed Him. Down even to death the blessed Saviour went. 'The depth closed Him round about.' For three days and nights He was 'in the heart of the earth' ... But God 'brought again from the dead our Lord Jesus'. On the third day Jonah came out on dry land. And on the third day Christ rose in triumph from the grave".

Notice that Jonah prayed only when he was in trouble. The Lord Jesus prayed in all circumstances. Read through Luke's Gospel, and make a list of the occasions on which the Saviour prayed.

Chapter 3: Greater than Jonah in His ministry

It was never said of the Lord Jesus, "And the word of the LORD came unto him ***the second time***, saying, Go unto Nineveh". Now we come to Jonah's eight-word sermon: "Yet forty days, and Nineveh shall be overthrown" (v.4). The dark cloud didn't have the slightest suggestion of a silver lining. Nineveh wasn't even urged to repent. Divine judgment was coming. Full stop! Micah would have frowned: "Who is a God like unto thee, that pardoneth iniquity, and passeth by the transgression of the remnant of his heritage? He retaineth not his anger for ever, because ***he delighteth in mercy***" (Micah 7:18). But that wasn't Jonah at all!

It is therefore with considerable relief that we turn to the New Testament. "For God sent not his Son into the world to condemn the world; but that the world through him might be saved" (John 3:17). Jonah would have found a kindred spirit in the disciples who called on the Lord to "command fire to come down from heaven, and consume them", but the Saviour said, "Ye know not what manner of spirit ye are of. For the Son of man is not come to ***destroy*** men's lives, but to ***save*** them" (Luke 9:51-56).

Jonah's preaching was limited in extent as well as content. He was sent to Nineveh. Simeon said, "Mine eyes have seen thy salvation, which thou hast prepared before the face of ***all people***" (Luke 2:30-31).

Chapter 4: Greater than Jonah in His mercy

Jonah evidently delighted in judgment. He failed to appreciate that it was God's "strange work … his strange act" (Isaiah 28:21). ("Strange" means 'alien'.) He failed to appreciate that God is "longsuffering to us-ward, not willing that any should perish, but that all should come to repentance" (2 Pet. 3:9).

The publican cried, "God be merciful to me a sinner (***'the*** sinner' JND)" (Luke 18:13). Blind Bartimaeus cried, "Jesus, thou Son of David, have mercy on me" (Mark 10:47). There was no reluctance on the part of the Saviour. It would have been a different story if Bartimaeus had cried to Jonah!

Jonah was very happy to say, "Salvation is of the LORD" (2:9), but not happy at all when God saved other people. He was very pleased to be saved himself, but had no concern about the teeming population of Nineveh. His message was in effect, "Get lost!"

Secondly, we can look at the prophecy of Jonah as:

B) A PICTURE OF ISRAEL

The book of Jonah must have a message for the time, otherwise it would be rather irrelevant. Its message to Israel is very clear indeed. The book of Jonah is most certainly a prophecy - it sets out the course of Israel's history.

i) Israel's mission

Jonah's commission to preach at Nineveh reminds us that Israel was entrusted with a mission to the nations. This was to display to the whole world the glory and ways of God. Israel should have been a object lesson to the whole world of the blessing which follows obedience to God. "This people have I formed for myself; they shall shew forth my praise" (Isaiah 43:21).

ii) Israel's transgression

Rather than obeying God, the nation went its own way and incurred divine wrath. See Isaiah 42 verses 24-25: "Who gave Jacob for a spoil, and Israel to the robbers? did not the LORD, he against whom we have sinned? for they would not walk in his ways, neither were they obedient unto his law.

Therefore he hath poured upon them the fury of his anger, and the strength of battle". See also Isaiah 48 verses 18-19, "O that thou hadst hearkened to my commandments! then had thy peace been as a river, and thy righteousness as the waves of the sea".

Notice two things:

a) Instead of bearing witness, Jonah went to Tarshish, one of the world's great commercial emporiums. Instead of bearing witness before the nations, Israel has made the acquisition of wealth her object. (What about us?)

b) Jonah's disobedience brought a storm on the Gentile mariners. Israel's disobedience has brought untold trouble on the Gentile nations. (Our disobedience can cause other people trouble too!)

iii) Israel's preservation

Like Jonah, Israel has been flung into the sea - a picture of the Gentile nations - but preserved in the sea. Protected and preserved from national obliteration, Israel remains a distinct people. See Revelation 12 verse 6, "And the woman fled into the wilderness, where she hath a place prepared of God". (See also Revelation 12:13-16.)

iv) Israel's resurrection

After passing through intense persecution, the nation will enjoy national resurrection. There will be a "third day" for Israel. See Hosea 6 verses 1-2: "After two days will he revive us: in the third day he will raise us up, and we shall live in his sight". (Read Isaiah 26:19.)

v) Israel's restoration

The nation will again be commissioned, and instead of shirking their ministry, they will fulfil it. Micah describes the future witness of Israel to the world: "And the remnant of Jacob shall be in the midst of many people as a dew from the LORD ... and the remnant of Jacob shall be among the Gentiles in the midst of many people as a lion among the beasts of the forest" (Micah 5:7-8). That is, the nation will be a blessing to those who receive their message, and judgment to those who do not. This coming missionary enterprise will be in the hands of Israel's Messiah: "I will also give thee for a light to the

Gentiles, that thou mayest be my salvation unto the end of the earth" (Isaiah 49:6). Paul said, "If the casting away of them be the reconciling of the world (i.e. divine blessing for the whole world through the Gospel), what shall the receiving of them be, ***but life from the dead*** (i.e. divine blessing for the whole world in the Millennium)" (Rom. 11:12-15).

vi) Israel's compassion

In that day, the nation will recognise God's interest and love for the Gentiles. See Isaiah 19 verses 23-25: "In that day shall there be a highway out of Egypt to Assyria, and the Assyrian shall come into Egypt, and the Egyptian into Assyria, and the Egyptians shall serve with the Assyrians. In that day shall Israel be the third with Egypt and with Assyria (its ancient capital was Nineveh), even a blessing in the midst of the land; whom the LORD of hosts shall bless, saying, Blessed be Egypt my people, and ***Assyria*** the work of my hands, and Israel mine inheritance".

Thirdly, we may look at the book of Jonah as:

C) A LESSON FOR OURSELVES

Here is a sample of the many practical lessons which will emerge as we proceed:

i) Disobedience brings discipline. We are required to obey God's word implicitly, else like Jonah we will go "down ... down ... down". We cannot escape God. "Whatsoever a man soweth, that shall he also reap."

ii) Repentance brings restoration. God does not disqualify us *ad infinitum*. How thankful we all are that He is willing to entrust His word to us for "the second time". How glad we are to hear David say, "He restoreth my soul".

iii) Resentment brings rebuke. We have to learn that God does not always work as we think He should. Sometimes, we are more severe than God.

The prophecy seems to end abruptly - almost in mid-air. But it is in this striking way that the Holy Spirit emphasises the mercy of God. He wishes us to leave the book of Jonah with this lesson firmly impressed on our hearts.

How much does the "love of Christ" constrain us?

JONAH

2) Read Chapter 1:1-10

We have already noticed that Jonah is described in 2 Kings 14 verse 25 as 'the LORD God of Israel's servant Jonah'. This is a very useful description to bear in mind as we tackle Jonah 1. The chapter may be divided as follows: ***(1)*** the servant's commission (vv.1-2); ***(2)*** the servant's disobedience (v.3); ***(3)*** the servant's discipline (vv.4-7); ***(4)*** the servant's confession (vv.8-10); ***(5)*** the servant's experience (vv.11-17).

1) THE SERVANT'S COMMISSION, vv.1-2

"Now the word of the LORD came unto Jonah the son of Amittai, saying, Arise, go to Nineveh, that great city, and cry against it; for their wickedness is come up before me."

The books of Jonah and Nahum remind us of the goodness and severity of God respectively (Rom. 11:22). The name "Jonah" means 'dove' – the symbol of peace, mildness and harmlessness. It was among the cheapest and commonest birds, reminding us that the "Prince of Peace" (Isa. 9:6) "became poor" that we "through his poverty might be rich" (2 Cor. 8:9).

Since the name "Amittai" is only mentioned in connection with Jonah (cf. 2 Kings 14:25), it can be safely assumed that reference is made to the same person in both cases. We know nothing of Amittai, so Jonah can be said to be the illustrious son of an unknown father, reminding us that a man's background is not a key factor in his service for God. It is where a man is going, rather than where he comes from, that is important.

We should notice that the words, "the word of the LORD came unto ...", are never used of the Lord Jesus. The word was in His heart at all times (Psalm 40:8).

a) The Lord made His will perfectly clear to Jonah

The prophet did not have to ask for guidance: he could not claim to be confused. He had to go personally. Nahum was also called to preach ***against*** Nineveh, but he was never told to preach ***in*** Nineveh. God uses His servants in different ways.

b) The Lord didn't give a range of options to Jonah

He didn't say, 'Jonah, perhaps you would like to consider visiting Nineveh'. Or, 'Jonah, give it some thought, and when you're ready …' It was a command, "Arise, Go to Nineveh …"

c) God spelt out the details for Jonah

"Arise, go to Nineveh, that great city, and cry against it; for their wickedness is come up before me."

i) "Arise." God did not expect His servant to be an 'armchair prophet'. He was required to expend some energy. Rather like Ezekiel: "Son of man, ***stand upon thy feet*** … I send thee … thou shalt speak my words unto them" (Ezek. 2:1-7). Let's face it, tracts are not given out and homes are not visited unless we "arise". Perhaps the words of the Lord Jesus are relevant in this context – "Take up thy bed and walk".

ii) "Go." This was not quite so easy as it sounds. First of all, it involved a journey of some five hundred miles across rugged country. Secondly, it took Jonah to the capital of a great enemy. Thirdly, it meant entering a vast city where he would be the only servant of God. This was a most intimidating prospect. Nineveh, located on the east bank of the River Tigris, is called "an exceeding great city of three days' journey" (Jonah 3:3). If you assume twenty miles for a day's journey, Nineveh would have been some sixty miles in extent. Today, we would use the expression 'Greater Nineveh'. It included its suburbs, one of which - Calah - was eighteen miles to the south of the actual capital. Even if you take the expression, "more than sixscore thousand persons" (Jonah 4:11), as Nineveh's population (it is often taken as the number of young children), it is a very daunting picture. One solitary servant of God amongst 120,000 Ninevites, whose reputation for cruelty was well-known. If you take the figure to refer to young children only, then you have a population of several million! Who said that the work of God was ever easy?!

But what about the command, "Go"? The Lord Jesus also said, "Go" (Matt. 28:19-20). In view of this, what about our 'Gospel Meetings'? One thing is sure: if our evangelism is limited to a meeting, then we are heading towards extinction. It's all too easy to sit comfortably in the hall on Sunday evenings, enjoying (hopefully!) what we hear, and forgetting that it can be the recipe for spiritual disaster. The old cry – 'evangelise or fossilise' - is not far wrong! Jonah refused to travel 500 miles: perhaps we baulk at walking 500 yards in the Lord's service. Our mission field is right on our doorstep, isn't it? Psalm 126 verse 6 is relevant here: "He that ***goeth forth*** and weepeth, bearing precious seed, shall doubtless come again with rejoicing, bringing his sheaves with him".

iii) "Cry." This just adds to the above. If Jonah had arrived in Nineveh with a nice comfortable message it might not have been so bad, but it wasn't that at all: ***"Cry against it."*** There was to be nothing half-hearted or apologetic about Jonah's preaching. He was to 'call aloud' or 'preach'. It was to be definite and forthright. God hated sin, and must judge sin. Compare the position of Nineveh with that of Sodom and Gomorrah. Apart from Lot and his family, God served no prior notice on "the cities of the plain".

Let's pause for a moment, and review the situation. We know from the end of the book that God intended to teach Jonah that it is so important to be right in attitude. Jonah even refused to go to Nineveh to "cry against it". His own welfare was far more important. We have an infinitely superior message to Jonah, but we do we care … ? What about our attitude?

2) THE SERVANT'S DISOBEDIENCE, v.3

"But Jonah rose up to flee unto Tarshish from the presence of the LORD." So he complied with the first part of God's instructions, "Arise". But that was about all! In fact, the next person to tell Jonah to "arise" was the shipmaster (v.6). It could be said that Jonah disobeyed the injunction, "Quench not the Spirit" (1 Thess. 5:19). There are at least four things to notice in this section:

i) Jonah purposed to "flee unto Tarshish". It would be an interesting exercise to look up the references to Tarshish. While the the name 'Tarshish' sometimes appears to be a descriptive name in the Old Testament, it is rather more definite here, and probably refers to Tartessus which was a copper-mining port in Spain. It was therefore as far westward as Nineveh was eastward. This speaks for itself.

ii) Jonah "went down to Joppa". He "went down" quite literally. He "***went down***" from the heights of Galilee to the coastal plain where Joppa (modern Jaffa) was situated; he "***went down***" into the ship; he "***went down*** to the bottoms of the mountains" (2:6). But he "went down" spiritually too, and so will we if we disobey God's word and reject His will.

In passing, we should note that another man (Peter) went to Joppa (in this case, 'up to Joppa', rather than 'down to Joppa': see Acts 9:38-39) and, initially, he too was averse to visiting the Gentiles: see Acts 10 verses 9-20. In the case of Jonah, we have a Jew who refused to overcome his prejudice against the Gentiles, whereas the Lord Jesus "must needs go through Samaria" (John 4:4). ("A greater than Jonas is here!", Matt. 12:41).

iii) Jonah "paid the fare thereof ... to go with them." It was all very deliberate. He evidently raided his bank account (or emptied his piggy bank) in order to secure safe passage to Tarshish and was not particularly worried about the company. He would rather "go with them" (idol-worshippers, v.5) than enjoy the Lord's presence. Compare Judas and Peter in John 18; they "stood with them" (vv.5, 18). It all proves, sadly, that disobedience clouds our judgment. After all, Jonah did know God. See again 2 Kings 14 verse 25. Jonah might have argued that since the circumstances were favourable, he was acting within the will of God. After all, the ship was there, he evidently had enough money to pay the fare, and all looked 'set fair' for his trip to Tarshish. But circumstances in themselves are no safe guide: we must have the word of the Lord.

iv) Jonah fled "from the presence of the LORD". The expression occurs three times: twice in verse 3 and again in verse 10. But was this possible? After all, David had said, "Whither shall I go from thy Spirit? or whither shall I flee from thy presence?" (Psalm 139:7-12). See again, 2 Kings 14 verse 25. The expression, "from the presence of the LORD", means more than His omnipresence, and can be best understood with reference to 1 Kings 17 verse 1, "As the Lord God of Israel liveth, ***before whom I stand***". Instead of moving consciously in the will of God, Jonah went elsewhere. It meant that he lost ***the joy*** of the Lord's presence.

3) THE SERVANT'S DISCIPLINE, vv.4-7

"But the LORD" (v.4). The section dealing with Jonah's disobedience commences with, "But Jonah". But (!) the prophet didn't have the last word.

How interesting! Why did God bother with Jonah? He could have easily sent someone else. After all, Jonah didn't seem to be very concerned about his disobedience. He was fast asleep in "the sides of the ship". The Lord Jesus slept through a storm for the simple reason that He knew He was acting at the time - and at every time - in the will of His Father. Jonah, the Lord's servant, slept whilst the heathen sailors prayed! His conscience didn't keep him awake. He seemed utterly insensitive to the situation. Even the storm didn't wake him. Whilst his journey had probably been quite exhausting, it's worth making the point that we're all capable of 'switching off' when there's something we don't want to hear, or don't want to do. We just try to shut God out. But, as we can see, God cannot be ignored:

i) Disobedience brings discipline. We must remember that Paul is writing to Christians in Galatians 6 verse 7, "Be not deceived; God is not mocked: for whatsoever a man soweth, that shall he also reap". God allowed Jonah to get very low - as far as "the sides of the ship" - before He began the process of restoration: and then He created a special situation to do it.

ii) Discipline is intended for our good. The storm was not an act of revenge, but the first stage in restoration. Let's face it, if God had immediately replaced Jonah with someone else, ***we would all have cause to worry***. After all, haven't we been disobedient too? But God wanted the very best for His servant, and had sent him to Nineveh, *inter alia,* for that purpose. He had some important lessons for His servant and took steps to ensure that Jonah learnt them.

iii) Disobedience does not alter God's will for us. Paul tells us that "the gifts and calling of God are without repentance" (Rom. 11:29). God carefully chooses His servants and does not easily set them aside.

iv) Disobedience brings problems for others. Christians in the wrong place always create problems for themselves and for the assemblies which they attend. Those poor mariners experienced a storm of exceptional strength. The Hebrew for "***sent out*** a great wind into the sea" means ***'hurled'*** or ***'flung*** out a great wind into the sea'. Read Acts 27, and you'll conclude that it's a whole lot better to have Paul, rather than Jonah, on board!

Do notice that the mariners only incurred further hardship by their delay in dealing with the problem as Jonah suggested. The only way in which Israel was delivered from further defeat was by dealing summarily with Achan. It was essential for the well-being of the assembly at Corinth that the guilty party was excommunicated. See 1 Corinthians 5.

This brings us to:

4) THE SERVANT'S CONFESSION, vv.8-10

Under interrogation, Jonah revealed that he was the cause of the storm (v.10). It was sad that he had to answer such a battery of questions. After all, people ought to be able to identify us from our life and conduct. The mariners had to drag the truth out of Jonah, but the Lord Jesus was able to say, "I spake openly to the world …" (John 18:20).

a) "What is thine occupation?"

We do not have a detailed reply from Jonah. He gives a general reply in verse 9. But we can answer for him, and for ourselves too. Jonah was the servant of God (2 Kings 14:25). We too are servants, but not only servants. The Lord Jesus said, "Henceforth I call you not servants; for the servant knoweth not what his lord doeth: but I have called you friends" (John 15:15). The question is, What kind of servants? Like this – "the servants of Christ, ***doing the will of God from the heart***?" (Eph. 6:6). Or like Jonah? He certainly didn't do the will of God "from the heart". In Chapter 1, he didn't do the will of God at all, and even when he was recommissioned, it seems highly unlikely that his heart was in his service. The Lord Jesus was so different: "Lo, I come: in the volume of the book it is written of me, I delight to do thy will, O my God: yea, thy law is within my heart" (Psalm 40:7-8). The Hebrew servant said, "I love my master, my wife, and my children; I will not go out free" (Exod. 21:5).

Let's get back to Ephesians 6 verse 6. Paul is actually referring to Christian slaves, but he calls them "the servants of Christ". So we are as much His servants when we are doing our daily work as we are when we are engaging in 'the Lord's work'. We are here primarily to serve God, and even our daily work should be regarded in this way. No employer could have better employees than that! When asked about his work, Wm. Carey replied that he was a 'servant of God, and cobbled shoes to pay expenses'.

Just look at the reward: "If any man serve me, let him follow me; and where I am, there shall also my servant be: if any man serve me, him will my Father honour" (John 12:26).

But Jonah was also a prophet. The business of a prophet was to "speak my word faithfully" (Jer. 23:28). He was a man, as we noticed in our introduction, who "stood in the counsel of the LORD, and hath perceived and heard his word" (Jer. 23:18). The Old Testament prophets, like the New Testament prophets, received their messages directly from God. That does not happen today. We do not have prophets now. The Word of God is complete. God does not speak to us ***directly***: He speaks to us ***through His written word***, that is, He speaks to us indirectly. But He does speak to us none the less, and we in turn are to 'speak His word faithfully'.

ii) "Whence comest thou?"

Well, Jonah was "the prophet, which was of Gath-hepher". What about us? The New Testament gives amazing answers to this question. For example: "According as he hath chosen us in him ***before the foundation of the world***" (Eph. 1:4). Or, "who hath saved us, and called us with an holy calling, not according to ***our*** works, but according to his own purpose and grace, which was given us in Christ Jesus ***before the world began*** (2 Tim. 1:9). Or, "called according to his purpose. For whom he did ***foreknow***, he also did predestinate to be conformed to the image of his Son ..." (Rom. 8:28-30). These and other wonderful statements fall into the category 'better felt than telt', as they say in Suffolk.

iii) "What is thy country?"

The Lord Jesus said, "My kingdom is not of this world" (John 18:36). Consequently, His subjects do not belong to this world either: "I have given them thy word; and the world hath hated them, because they are not of the world, even as I am not of the world" (John 17:14-16). Well, what is our country? Paul gives us the answer in Philippians 3 verse 20: "For our conversation (citizenship) ***is in heaven***". That's where we belong, and that's where we're going: "to an inheritance incorruptible, and undefiled, and that fadeth not away, reserved in ***heaven*** for you" (1 Pet. 1:4). We are "partakers of the ***heavenly*** calling" (Heb. 3:1).

This, of course, regulates our position in the world. Peter again: "Dearly beloved, I beseech you as strangers and pilgrims" (1 Pet. 2:11). We are "strangers" to earth and "pilgrims" to heaven. As "strangers", we are ***away from home***: as "pilgrims", we are ***going home.*** But what else? Paul now: "Now then we are ambassadors for Christ, as though God did beseech by us: we pray in Christ's stead, be ye reconciled to God" (2 Cor. 5: 20), omitting the AV italics to get the right sense!

I am a stranger here, within a foreign land;
My home is far away, upon a golden strand.
Ambassador to be, of realms beyond the sea;
I'm here on business for my King.

iv) "Of what people art thou?"

Jonah answers this one himself: "I am an Hebrew". Why didn't he say, 'I am an Israelite'? According to *Unger's Commentary on the Old Testament*: 'He did not employ the term Israelite, for that designation was employed among themselves, with Hebrew used among non-Israelites'. You had better check that out for yourself - and share your conclusions. He might have said something like, "And what one nation in the earth is like, ***thy people***, even like Israel, whom God went to redeem for a people to himself?" (2 Sam. 7:23).

We belong to a unique people. Not a national group, but a people where "there is neither Greek nor Jew, circumcision nor uncircumcision, Barbarian, Scythian, bond nor free: but Christ is all, and in all" (Col. 3.11). See also 1 Peter 2 verses 9-10. Note the expression, "a ***peculiar people***" ('a people for a possession'), and the statement, "which in time past ***were not a people***, but are ***now the people of God***". Don't forget the practical side: "A peculiar people, ***zealous of good works***" (Titus 2:14).

As we have already noticed, Jonah answered all four questions in one sentence: "I am an Hebrew; and I fear the LORD, the God of heaven, which hath made the sea and the dry land" (v.9). Taken by themselves, these are noble words indeed. But taken in context, they seem rather empty, as the mariners were quick to point out: "Why hast thou done this? ('How could you do this?' NASB) For the men knew that he fled from the presence of the LORD, because he had told them". What's more, it wasn't Jonah's fellow-Hebrews who said this; it was the pagan sailors. What a terrible loss of testimony! Jonah's profession was not matched by his practice. If he really feared the Lord, why had he disobeyed Him? If he really believed in "the

God of heaven, which hath made the sea and the dry land", why had he attempted to flee from Him? Pagan religions spawned separate gods for heaven, sea, and earth. But the existence of only one God meant that there was no possibility of escape from Him. So why had he tried? All we can say is that Jonah at least had the moral courage to admit that he was wrong.

But it isn't unknown for people to say, 'How could you - ***a Christian*** - do this?' Whilst, as the following verses show, God's name was not brought into disrepute through Jonah's behaviour, Paul did have to say later, "For the name of God is blasphemed among the Gentiles through you (Jews)" (Rom. 2:24). ***It should be quite unthinkable that we could be guilty of this too.***

JONAH

3) Read Chapter 1:11-17

In our previous study, we suggested that this chapter may be divided as follows: ***(1)*** the servant's commission (vv.1-2); ***(2)*** the servant's disobedience (v.3); ***(3)*** the servant's discipline (vv.4-7); ***(4)*** the servant's confession (vv.8-10); ***(5)*** the servant's experience (vv.11-17). Having considered the first four sections, we come now to:

5) THE SERVANT'S EXPERIENCE, vv.11-17

The mariners were full of questions, and it certainly wasn't idle curiosity! Their questions fell into three categories:

i) About Jonah personally. "What is thine occupation? and whence comest thou? what is thy country? and of what people art thou?" (v.8).

ii) About Jonah's conduct. "Why hast thou done this?" (v.10).

iii) About Jonah's future. "What shall we do unto thee?" (v.11).

We have already answered the battery of questions put to Jonah in verse 8, but it might be helpful to give a little more consideration to the question in verse 10, "Why hast thou done this?" Jonah tells us in Chapter 4 why he went "with them unto Tarshish from the presence of the LORD" (1:3). The prophet is "displeased" and "very angry" (4:1): "Therefore I fled before unto Tarshish: for I knew that thou art a gracious God, and merciful, slow to anger, and of great kindness, and repentest thee of the evil" (4:2). But how could this prompt Jonah to flee? You would have thought that he would have been delighted that God withheld judgment.

Nineveh was the capital of Assyria, the very nation which would ultimately sweep Israel (the northern of the two kingdoms into which God's people were divided at that time) into captivity. Israel was in dire straits when Jeroboam II came to the throne: "For the LORD saw the affliction of Israel, that it was very bitter: for there was not any shut up, nor any left, nor any helper for Israel" (2 Kings 14:26). Through Jonah, God promised deliverance, and restoration of territory. Now comes the irony of the situation so far as Jonah was concerned. He is sent to the people who posed the biggest threat to Israel, and he knows very well that if the Ninevites repent, God will exercise mercy. But Jonah doesn't want them to repent. If Nineveh perished, then Israel might be saved. So he decides not to go: Nineveh would not then have any opportunity to repent, and God's wrath would fall on the city.

Jonah thought it out very carefully. He counted the cost in money and safety (vv.3, 12), and paid the fare for a passage to Tarshish, all because he loved Israel and wanted their deliverance. He sacrificed himself, misguidedly, to save his people. Well, he was misguided, ***but the "Greater than Jonah" gave Himself to save His people, and it was according to "the determinate counsel and foreknowledge of God" (***Acts 2:23).

Now we come to the question put to Jonah in verse 11: "Then said they unto him, What shall we do unto thee, that the sea may be calm unto us? for the sea wrought, and was tempestuous". Jonah was powerless to control the wind and sea, but the Lord Jesus (always "greater than Jonas") "rebuked the wind, and said unto the sea, Peace, be still. And the wind ceased, and there was a great calm" (Mark 4:39).

We may approach this section of the prophecy in three ways:

a) What Jonah did, v.12

He requested to be thrown overboard. "Take me up, and cast me forth into the sea; so shall the sea be calm unto you: for I know that for my sake this great tempest is upon you." (The sailors knew that Jonah was willing to die in order to save their lives.)

We are reminded here that the "greater than Jonas" said, "Therefore doth my Father love me, because I lay down my life, that I might take it again. No man taketh it from me, but I lay it down of myself. I have power to lay it down, and I have power to take it again. This commandment have I received of my Father" (John 10:17-18).

We should notice at least two things here:

i) Jonah was willing to sacrifice himself to preserve others. We have already thought about this so far as Israel was concerned. Jonah would go as far as death to ensure that Nineveh never heard God's word, and would therefore perish. But his death would also mean safety and preservation for the terrified sailors. Although he was misguided, it is difficult to escape the sincerity of his motives. He was willing to lose his life for others. ***What about us?***

Paul described the sacrificial concern of the Macedonian Christians like this: "For to their power (their ability), I bear record, yea, and beyond their power (their ability) they were willing of themselves" (2 Cor. 8:3). They went right to the breadline, and beyond it, in order to help the needy saints in Judaea. This is how John puts it: "Hereby perceive we the love of God, because he laid down his life for us: and we ought to lay down our lives for the brethren" (1 John 3:16). How much do we really care about other Christians, or about the unsaved?

ii) Jonah recognised others were suffering through his disobedience. "I know that for ***my sake*** this great tempest is upon you." This happened in the battle against Ai: "And Joshua said (to Achan), Why hast thou ***troubled us?***" (Joshua 7:25). We are not like a modern ship with separate water-tight compartments. We are "members one of another". We have a decided influence on each other, whether for good or for bad. Our disobedience, or lack of spirituality, will affect the whole assembly.

But we can have a harmful influence on each other by doing something that is not wrong in itself! "But if thy brother be grieved with thy meat, now walkest thou not charitably. Destroy not him with thy meat, for whom Christ died" (Rom. 14:15). The passage teaches that there may be certain things which, while not in any way sinful in themselves, could trouble the consciences of others. In that case, love for them should make us forego our own interests to ensure that fellow-believers are not disturbed or offended. We are not to "please ourselves", but to consider others (Rom. 15:1-3). Paul is speaking here about eating meat previously offered to idols, but can you think of circumstances in which the principle applies today?

b) What the mariners did, vv.13-16

Incidentally, the word for "mariners" (v.5) is actually, 'salts'! We should notice four things:

i) They "rowed hard". But why did they have to row? The answer lies in verse 5: they "cast forth the wares that were in the ship into the sea, to lighten it of them". The "wares" were not the cargo, but the ship's tackle.

You have got to admit that these heathen sailors did their very best to save Jonah. "The men rowed hard to bring it to the land." They could have taken him at his word, and heaved him overboard immediately. But they acted very mercifully toward the man who had caused them so much trouble. We must give them full marks for trying. Like the disciples on Galilee, they were "toiling in rowing; for the wind was contrary unto them" (Mark 6:48).

All of which reminds us of the need for perseverance in the Christian life. Are we still 'rowing hard' in prayer for backsliders? Are we still 'rowing hard' in prayer for unsaved members of the family? Are we still 'rowing hard' in prayer for colleagues at work? Are we still 'rowing hard' in prayer for people in the streets around us? Whilst all ***their*** effort proved vain, ***we*** do have the promise: "And let us not be weary in well doing: for in due season we shall reap, if we faint not" (Gal. 6:9). (But do have a look at the context of this quotation.)

Christian service is very much a case of:

Toiling on! ... Toiling on! ...
Toiling on! ... Toiling on! ...
Let us hope, ... Let us watch ...,
And labour till the Master comes.

ii) They "cried unto the LORD", v.14. This represents an enormous improvement in their outlook. Previously, they "cried every man unto his god" (v.5). Their cry reflects some very intelligent thinking. They evidently believed that God would not act in an arbitrary way, and condemn the guiltless. We know that David frequently appealed to the Lord on this very basis. See, for example, Psalm 26 verse 9 and 28 verse 9. They also believed in God's irresistible power – "for thou, O LORD, hast done as it pleased thee" (v.14).

The words of the sailors - "Lay not upon us innocent blood" - remind us that Pilate said, "I am innocent of the blood of this just person" (Matt.27:24), and that Judas Iscariot used similar language: "I have sinned in that I have betrayed the innocent blood" (Matt. 27:4).

To whom do ***we*** cry, and where do ***we*** place our trust? There are plenty of gods in Western civilisation. Psalm 147 reminds us that God "delighteth not in the strength of the horse: he taketh not pleasure in the legs of a man" (v.10). But plenty of people do just that. "The strength of the horse" is the be-all and end-all on Derby Day, and in the betting shops (the 'Turf Accountants' - have you ever heard such a slur on the accountancy profession?). "The legs of a man" are the objects of wholesale idolatry, especially when they've got football boots at the bottom! People, including Christians, still cry "every man unto his god". The Bible says, "Little children, keep yourselves from idols" (1 John 5:21). Do we ***really*** trust in the Lord?

iii) They "took up Jonah, and cast him forth into the sea". In verse 5, the ship's equipment had been "cast .... into the sea", but that hadn't solved the problem. Although they had been told how to deal with the situation, they tried to grapple with the result of the problem, rather than the cause, by endeavouring to row out of difficulty, but that hadn't helped either. In the end, the sailors were forced to deal with the cause of their difficulties.

Sadly, we are often like these seafarers. We will do anything and everything to lessen the effect of our spiritual ineffectiveness, rather than tackle the source. The only way out for the sailors was to consign the problem to death, and that is exactly what we must do too: "***Mortify*** (put to death) therefore your members which are upon the earth; fornication, uncleanness, inordinate affection, evil concupiscence, and covetousness, which is idolatry" (Col. 3:5).

Strangely enough, there was something almost tender in the way Jonah was thrown overboard! The words, "so they ***took up*** Jonah", come from a Hebrew word which suggests great care. It is used in Isaiah 40 verse 11, "He shall gather the lambs with his arm, and carry them in his bosom". Perhaps they were rather reluctant to jettison Jonah in this way, and perhaps we too are rather reluctant to eject those things in our lives which cause spiritual weakness.

iv) They "feared the LORD exceedingly, and offered a sacrifice unto the LORD, and made vows", v.16. Compare Mark 4 verse 41, "And they (the Lord's disciples) feared exceedingly, and said one to another, What manner of man is this, that even the wind and the sea obey him?"

If heathen mariners responded like this, what about us? They had seen striking evidence of God's power: we have striking evidence of His love as well as His power. The Old Testament has a great deal to say about "the fear of the Lord". Amongst other things, "the fear of the Lord" describes a great reverence for Him. What kind of sacrifice should we make? Romans 12 verse 1 supplies part of the answer. What about vows? It is, of course, very much an Old Testament subject, to which even Acts 18 verse 18 and 21 verse 23 (the two N.T. references) refer back. See, for example, the vow of the Nazarite in Numbers 6. Should ***we*** make vows? Our whole life should be consecrated to God. We should all be marked by resolution and determination to do His will at all times, and to serve Him constantly.

c) What the Lord did, v.17

"Now the LORD had prepared a great fish to swallow up Jonah. And Jonah was in the belly of the fish three days and three nights." God prepares four things in the book of Jonah. The "great fish", the "gourd", the "worm", and the "vehement east wind" (4:6-8). However, the word "prepare" does not mean to create: rather, to appoint or assign. So we are not obliged to think that the "great fish" was a specially created specimen. Whilst in the New Testament the word rendered "whale" means 'a huge fish or sea monster' (W.E. Vine), it could easily have been a whale. Sperm whales are capable of swallowing a man, and inhabited the Mediterranean in past centuries. So we have no problem at all in singing:

Listen to my tale
Of Jonah and the whale,
Way down in the middle of the ocean.

The Lord Jesus said two quite different things about Jonah. First of all, there was "the sign of the prophet Jonas". See Matthew 12 verses 39-41, but in particular, "For as Jonas was three days and three nights in the whale's belly; so shall the Son of man be three days and three nights in the heart of the earth". Secondly, "For as Jonas was a sign unto the Ninevites, so shall also the Son of man be to this generation" (Luke 11:30). The first refers to Jonah's experience: the second to the distinctiveness of his witness in Nineveh. It is the first of these which we must now consider.

i) What about the "three days and three nights"? This is usually explained with reference to the Hebrew custom of treating part days as full days. If the Lord had said, "three days", without reference to nights, there would be no dispute. In that way, you can make Good Friday fit with Easter Sunday! But the Lord Jesus was very specific – "three days ***and three nights***". Compare Esther 4 verse 16, "Fast ye for me, and neither eat nor drink ***three days, night or day***". Also 1 Samuel 30 verse 12, "He had eaten no bread, nor drunk any water, ***three days and three nights***". This raises an immediate question: when was the Lord crucified? Is Good Friday inaccurate? See the addendum.

ii) Where did Jonah actually go? It has been suggested that since the Lord Jesus referred to Jonah's experience in speaking about His own death, Jonah must have died. His terrifying experience might well have made him imagine that he was actually dead: witness his words, "in the belly of hell". But it seems unnecessary to go beyond the fact that Jonah's disappearance was a figure of the Lord's disappearance, when His body was placed in the grave.

ADDENDUM

"Three days and three nights in the heart of the earth"

1. The Lord Jesus was crucified at 09.00 on Thursday, and died at 15.00.

2. He was placed in Joseph's tomb by the commencement of the sabbath i.e. prior to 18.00 on Thursday = 1 Day

3. He was in the tomb from 18.00 on Thursday to 06.00 on Friday = 1 Night.

4. He was in the tomb from 06.00 on Friday to 18.00 on Friday = 1 Day.

5. He was in the tomb from 18.00 on Friday to 06.00 on Saturday = 1 Night

6. He was in the tomb from 06.00 on Saturday to 18.00 on Saturday = 1 Day.

7. He was in the tomb from 18.00 on Saturday to, say, 06.00 on Sunday = 1 night.

The last time is confirmed by Matthew 27 verse 28, "Now late on sabbath, as it was the dusk of the next day after sabbath" (JND). See also Luke 24 verse 1, "But on the morrow of the sabbath, very early indeed in the morning …" (JND). The Jewish sabbath ended at 18.00, and, obviously, the women would not come at night: they waited until "very early in the morning the first day of the week" (Mark 16:2).

But if the Jews would not allow the body to remain on the cross "on the sabbath day" (i.e. the day commencing at 18.00 on Friday), surely the Lord must have been crucified on Friday prior to this time. The argument for crucifixion on Thursday must therefore be faulty. But do notice that John 19 verse 31 gives us a little more information: "***for that sabbath was an high day***". The Jews adjusted their calendar to ensure that 14th Nisan never fell on the Sabbath, and in this case, the 14th Nisan was itself treated as a Sabbath: "ye shall do no servile work therein" (Lev. 23:7). This was the "high day". So both the day commencing 18.00 on Thursday (the "high day") and the day commencing 18.00 on Friday (the actual sabbath) were regarded as sabbath days.

However, Mark tells us that the Lord Jesus "was risen early the first day of the week" (Mark 16:9). Does this mean, bearing in mind that the first day of the week commenced at 18.00 on Saturday, that we should start working back from that time? That is, the period ends with the last of the three ***days.***

While not all are agreed on the precise timing of events here, we must never forget the wonderful fact that, "He is risen, as he said" (Matt. 28:6).

JONAH

4) Read Chapter 2:1-10

As we have seen in previous studies, Jonah's experience was a picture of the death and resurrection of the Lord Jesus. This enables us to say, without stretching the passage, that Jonah ultimately arrived in the Assyrian capital having symbolically passed through death and resurrection. In a very real way, Jonah went "into death" and was "raised up" to "walk in newness of life" (Rom. 6:4). He certainly 'died' to his disobedience, and 'rose' to a new relationship with God. But it was a most painful experience for him. We too must face the fact that whilst there is great joy in doing the Lord's will, it is often preceded by painful sacrifice. We do like our own way, don't we? What's more, it takes most of us some time to deal ruthlessly with our own way and our own will. Read the end of Jonah 1 and the beginning of Jonah 2, without stopping. "And Jonah was in the belly of the fish three days and three nights. ***Then*** Jonah prayed unto the LORD his God out of the fish's belly." This suggests that it was three days and three nights before Jonah came finally to absolute trust in God, and devotion to His will.

The chapter may be divided as follows: ***(1)*** the circumstances of Jonah's prayer (v.1); ***(2)*** the acceptance of Jonah's prayer (v.2); ***(3)*** the understanding in Jonah's prayer (v.3); ***(4)*** the thanksgiving in Jonah's prayer (vv.3-7); ***(5)*** the resolve in Jonah's prayer (vv.8-9); ***(6)*** the result of Jonah's prayer (v.10).

1) THE CIRCUMSTANCES OF JONAH'S PRAYER, v.1

We have all probably prayed in unusual places, but nothing to rival this: "Then Jonah prayed unto the LORD his God out of the fish's belly" (v.1). It would be quite illuminating to make a list of the different places and circumstances in the Bible in which people prayed.

It all goes to emphasise that we can approach God in all circumstances and at all times, always bearing in mind the psalmist's words, "If I regard iniquity in my heart, the Lord will not hear me" (Psalm 66:18). But if that is the case, why did God hear Jonah? After all, this was the man who fled "from the presence of the LORD" in his disobedience. But as we will see from this chapter, the disobedient prophet faced up to his disobedience, and God recommissioned him for service at Nineveh. We cannot go any further without remembering that the "greater than Jonah" said, "My meat is to do the will of him that sent me, and to finish his work" (John 4:34), and "He that hath sent me is with me: the Father hath not left me alone; for I do always those things that please him" (John 8:29).

This is the first occasion in the book on which Jonah prayed, even though the "shipmaster" had urged him to do so (1:6). There is no reference to him praying in Chapter 1, which reminds us that prayer is the first thing to go when we are out of fellowship with God. The mariners had "cried every man unto his god" (1:5), and the shipmaster had told Jonah to do the same: "What meanest thou, O sleeper? arise, call upon thy God" (1:6). Now, at long last, he turns to God in prayer.

The contrast between Jonah and the Lord Jesus could not be more distinct. This is emphasised particularly in Luke's Gospel. See, for example, Luke 3 verse 21: "Now when all the people were baptized, it came to pass, that Jesus also being baptized, ***and praying*** ..." Only Luke records the fact that the Lord prayed here. Luke emphasises the perfect humanity, or manhood, of the Lord Jesus and therefore His dependence upon God. He prays repeatedly in Luke. He prayed at the commencement of His service (as noted) and at the completion of His redeeming work: "Father, into thy hands I commend my spirit" (23:46). He prayed on a mountain in connection with His glory (9:29), and in a valley in connection with His agony (22:41). He prayed in popularity (5:15-16) and in adversity (23:34). He prayed for an entire night (6:12) before choosing His disciples. (See also 11:1; 22:32.)

Jonah prayed to the "LORD ***his*** God". Since this was the case, it might be asked, how could Jonah's God possibly allow him to get into a situation like that? Was He really the God of Jonah? The answer is, of course, that the Lord actually put Jonah inside the great fish, ***because He was Jonah's God***. If He wasn't, Jonah would have perished in the Mediterranean. In using the words, "the LORD ***his*** God", Jonah recognised that God was dealing with him for his good, and was not intent on his destruction. This was proved by the fact that he was in the "fish's belly", and not dead in the sea. In fact, he was sane enough to pray! It might be helpful at this stage to read Hebrews 12 verses 1-13, although we should bear in mind that, strictly speaking, the chastening described there is not related to sin.

Although disobedient and chastened, Jonah retained a sense of relationship with God. Sin interrupts fellowship with God, but not the relationship with God.

2) THE ACCEPTANCE OF JONAH'S PRAYER, v.2

"Then Jonah prayed unto the LORD his God ... and said, I cried by reason of mine affliction unto the LORD, ***and he heard me***; out of the belly of hell ('the grave', AV margin) cried I, ***and thou heardest my voice."***

Before continuing, we should pause to remember that of the "greater than Jonas" it was said, "Who in the days of his flesh, when he had offered up prayers and supplications with strong crying and tears unto him that was able to save him from death … was ***heard*** in that he feared ('because of his piety', JND)" (Heb. 5:7). He was able to say, "Father, I thank thee that thou hast heard me. And I knew that ***thou hearest me always***: but because of the people which stand by I said it, that they may believe that thou hast sent me" (John 11:41-42). We must not forget, however, that at Calvary, He cried, "O my God, I cry in the daytime, but ***thou hearest not***; and in the night season, and am not silent" (Psalm 22:2).

Returning now to the passage before us, it should be noted that Jonah uses the ***past*** tense: "He heard me … thou heardest my voice". This requires some explanation. After all, Jonah was still in the "the fish's belly" (v.1). He had not yet been delivered. The answer lies in the fact that the chapter refers to two stages in Jonah's deliverance. When Jonah prayed, the ***first*** had already taken place, and the ***second*** was about to take place.

- The first had already taken place. Jonah's prayer ***refers principally to his deliverance from death by drowning.*** Read the prayer through carefully, and you will see that it is really a prayer of ***thanksgiving***. Jonah tells us about his experience, and punctuates his story with thanksgiving to God for hearing and delivering him. He tells us in his prayer that he had ***already*** cried to the Lord for deliverance, and that the Lord had both heard and answered him. "I cried by reason of my affliction unto the LORD, and he heard me; out of the belly of hell cried I, and thou heardest my voice" (v.2); "When my soul fainted within me I remembered the LORD: and my prayer came in unto thee, into thine holy temple" (v.7). Jonah is referring to prayer already made, and expressing his thanks to the Lord for hearing him. When he reached the bottom of the sea (v.6), it must have seemed to him that he was in his grave. In the Old Testament, the word *Sheol* (translated 'hell' here, AV) refers to the realm of the dead generally. But God had saved him from a 'watery grave' by sending a submarine (the whale) to retrieve him!

- The second was about to take place. It actually took place at the end of the chapter. "And the LORD spake unto the fish, and it vomited out Jonah upon the dry land" (v.10).

But why had God answered Jonah's cry? Jonah's experiences had brought him to see the folly of his ways, and made him turn to God in his distress. It was because Jonah had "a right spirit" (Psalm 51:10), that he was able to say, "he heard me".

We are reminded by John, "This is the confidence that we have in him, that, if we ask any thing according to his will, ***he heareth us***" (1 John 5:14). God tells us that "to this man will I look, even to him that is poor and of a contrite spirit, and trembleth at my word" (Isaiah 66:2).

3) THE UNDERSTANDING IN JONAH'S PRAYER, v.3

Jonah was deeply conscious that he was not the victim of blind fate. His circumstances were divinely designed. Jonah said, "I cried by reason of mine affliction unto the LORD" (v.2), because he realised that the Lord had caused that affliction: "For ***thou*** hadst cast me into the deep, in the midst of the seas; and the floods compassed me about; all ***thy*** billows and ***thy*** waves passed over me" (v.3). (Job and David also made similar statements; see Job 1:21 with 2:10, and 2 Samuel 16:10.) So both the sailors and the sea were God's servants. The sailors that "took up Jonah, and cast him forth into the sea" (1:15), were actually employed by God. The sea which "wrought, and was tempestuous" (1:11), was equally a servant of God. The very storm itself was initiated by God (1:4). Jonah realised that God had taken steps, drastic steps, to recover His servant. Sometimes, like Jonah, we have to go down, down, down, before, like the prodigal son, we 'come to ourselves'. If things seem to be going terribly wrong in your life, just ask yourself if God is speaking to you. When things go wrong, it does not necessarily mean that you have caused Him displeasure - but then, you will know only too well whether or not that is the case.

Paul was able to look intelligently at his unpleasant circumstances, and say, "I would ye should understand, brethren, that the things which happened unto me have fallen out rather unto the furtherance of the gospel" (Phil. 1:12). He could also talk about "a thorn in the flesh, the messenger of Satan to buffet me, lest I should be exalted above measure" (2 Cor.12:7). In both cases, Paul discerned the hand of God in his life.

Let's stop for a moment and look again at Jonah's language. He is quoting Psalm 42 verse 7 ("Deep calleth unto deep at the noise of thy waterspouts: all thy waves and thy billows are gone over me"). He evidently also refers to Psalm 69 verses 1-2, 14-15 ("Save me, O God; for the waters are come in unto my soul. I sink in deep mire, where there is no standing: I am come into deep waters, where the floods overflow me ... Deliver me out of the mire, and let me not sink: let me be delivered from them that hate me, and out of the deep waters. Let not the waterflood overflow me, neither let the deep swallow me up, and let not the pit shut her mouth upon me"). These Psalms point us to the Lord Jesus. While He was "taken, and by wicked hands ... crucified, and slain", it was in "the determinate counsel and foreknowledge of God" (Acts 2:23). The Lord Jesus experienced the "waves" and "billows" of divine judgment at Calvary: "Awake, O sword, against my shepherd, and against the man that is my fellow, saith the LORD of hosts: smite the shepherd, and the sheep shall be scattered ...." (Zech. 13:7; Mark 14:27).

We should notice how Jonah describes his terrifying experiences. He appears to do this in three stages, but not without interjecting thanksgiving for deliverance. So:

4) THE THANKSGIVING IN JONAH'S PRAYER, vv.3-7

It is noteworthy that even in the midst of his horrifying experience, Jonah did not forget the Scriptures. See above. It was so with the Lord Jesus. See, for example, John 19 verse 28, "Jesus knowing that all things were now accomplished, that the scripture might be fulfilled, saith, I thirst". See Psalm 69 verse 21.

As suggested above, Jonah was evidently thankful in each stage of his terrifying experience:

Stage 1: Into the sea, vv.3-4

"For thou hadst cast me into the deep, in the midst of the seas; and the floods compassed me about: all thy billows and thy waves passed over me. Then I said, I am cast out of thy sight; ***yet I will look again toward thy holy temple***" (vv.3-4). You can see very clearly how Jonah was affected by his terrifying ordeal: "Then I said, ***I am cast out of thy sight***". This was the man who "rose up to flee … from the presence of the LORD". Now he has to confess that there was nothing quite so dreadful as being away from God! There should be nothing so dreadful to ***us*** than distance from Christ. We must take all necessary steps to ensure that if something mars our fellowship with Him, the matter is dealt with immediately. Our union with Christ can never be destroyed: but our communion with Him can so easily be interrupted.

Jonah's sense of distance from God gives place to renewed confidence: "***Yet I will look again toward thy holy temple***". This does not mean just looking in the right direction in the same way that Moslems look toward Mecca! It means waiting again on God for direction and guidance. What brought about the dramatic change in verse 4? God's dealings with Jonah had been effective, and the prophet had turned to Him in repentance and faith.

Stage 2: Down to the bottom, vv.5-6

"The waters compassed me about, even to the soul: the depth closed me round about, the weeds were wrapped about my head. I went down to the bottoms of the mountains; the earth with her bars was about me for ever: ***yet hast thou brought up my life from corruption (the pit), O LORD my God***" (vv.5-6). Notice again how the story is punctuated with thanksgiving.

We have a graphic picture of a drowning man. He even describes the entangling seaweed. Down he goes, right to the bottom - to the point at which the mountains rise from the sea bed - and he is trapped beyond hope: "the earth with her bars was about me for ever". It has been suggested (M. Unger) that this describes the 'craggy subterranean rocks' which prevented him from getting back to the safety of land.

Now remember, Jonah was still in the fish's belly when he said, "But thou hast brought up my life from the pit, O Jehovah my God" (v.6, JND). He had been ***saved from drowning*** through divine intervention. God's 'submarine' arrived exactly at the right time! We too have been saved from death by divine intervention. Jonah now speaks in the first person, as opposed to the third person in verse 1, when he says, "Yet hast thou brought up my life from corruption, O LORD ***my*** God". He is deeply conscious of God's personal interest in him and concern for him. Paul could say, "But ***my*** God shall supply all your need according to his riches in glory by Christ Jesus" (Phil. 4:19). On the other hand, the words, "O LORD ***my*** God", may well suggest Jonah's devotion to Him.

Stage 3: About to die, v.7

"When my soul fainted within me I remembered the LORD: and ***my prayer came in unto thee, into thine holy temple***" (v.7). It isn't at all easy to pinpoint the exact moment at which Jonah felt his life ebbing away. Was it before the fish swallowed him, or during his stay in the fish's belly? If anything, the latter seems more likely in view of verse 2, but Jonah had reached the point of death. He had come to the end, and it was at that point that he "remembered the Lord" from whose presence he had fled. Sometimes God has to bring us to the end of ourselves before we turn to Him. See, again, the prodigal son, "And when he came to himself, he said, How many hired servants of my father's have bread enough and to spare, and I perish with hunger! I will arise and go to my father" (Luke 15:17-18).

Whilst Jonah's experience was the direct result of his disobedience, God sometimes brings us through circumstances calculated to make us trust Him more. Rather like Peter as he was "beginning to sink", we have to cry in our extremity, "Lord, save me" (Matt. 14:30), and rather like Paul who wrote, "But we had the sentence of death in ourselves, that we should not trust in ourselves, but in God which raiseth the dead" (2 Cor. 1:9).

We must remember that the physical and spiritual sufferings of the "greater than Jonas" were occasioned by His unqualified obedience to the will of God. Jonah suffered because of his sin. The Lord Jesus was sinless. Jonah suffered because of his disobedience. The Lord Jesus suffered because of His obedience. See Philippians 2 verse 8: He "became obedient unto death, even the death of the cross". The weeds were wrapped around Jonah's head. The Lord Jesus wore a crown of thorns. Jonah cried, "I am cast out of thy sight". The Lord Jesus cried, "My God, my God, why hast thou forsaken me?" (Matt. 27:46).

5) THE RESOLVE IN JONAH'S PRAYER, vv.8-9

"They that observe lying vanities forsake their own mercy. But I will sacrifice unto thee with the voice of thanksgiving; I will pay that I have vowed. Salvation is of the LORD." The "lying vanities" are 'vain idols' (JND margin). In the context of the book of Jonah, this must refer to the idolatrous mariners who "cried every man unto his god", and got nowhere. See Chapter 1 verse 5. But what about the words, "forsake their own ***mercy***"? Once again, the JND footnote looks helpful and gives "mercy" as grace or favour. This gives the sense of the statement as something like, 'They that revere worthless idols give up the grace available to them'. But is Jonah merely condemning idolatry as it stands, or is he implying that he had turned to idolatrous men for assistance as he fled from God? The latter seems more likely. We must be careful whose advice and guidance we seek.

Jonah now distances himself from such practices, whether by others, or by himself in this case:

i) "***I will*** sacrifice ***unto thee*** (not 'vain idols') with the voice of thanksgiving" (v.9). He thought of the Lord's mercy and grace in preserving his life, and did what we all must do: "Therefore let us offer the sacrifice of praise to God continually, that is, the fruit of our lips, giving thanks to his name" (Heb. 13:15).

ii) "***I will*** pay that that I have vowed." M.F. Unger's comment seems most appropriate here: 'His spirit contrasts with many who make vows when brought face to face with death, as he had been, which they promptly forget when the danger has passed'. Do we really mean what we sometimes sing:

"O Jesus, I have promised to serve Thee to the end."

The Lord Jesus did not need to make vows. He said, "I have set the LORD always before me ..." (Psalm 16:8).

6) THE RESULT OF JONAH'S PRAYER, v.10

His prayer reaches its climax with, "***Salvation is of the Lord***". Then, and only then, do we read, "And the LORD spake unto the fish, and it vomited out Jonah upon the dry land". Jonah loses all sight of himself and recognises that deliverance was God's prerogative. The man who "went down" only 'came up' when he started to look in the right direction! No way could he extricate himself from the fish's belly: he was obliged to rely solely upon God for salvation. Once he had completely turned to God in this way, as we all do for salvation, he was delivered. He arrives on dry ground, ready to hear God's voice "the second time" (3:1) as a man who had passed through death and resurrection. The old and disobedient Jonah was finished, and a new man stepped forward to serve God.

The deliverance of Jonah reminds us that the Lord Jesus "offered up prayers and supplications with strong crying and tears unto him that was able to save him from (*ek,* 'out of') death, and was heard in that he feared ('because of his piety', JND)" (Heb. 5:7).

JONAH

5) Read Chapter 3:1-10

Whilst in the "fish's belly", Jonah had cried, "I will sacrifice unto thee with the voice of thanksgiving; ***I will pay that that I have vowed***" (2:9). Perhaps Jonah remembered that Solomon had said, "When thou vowest a vow unto God, defer not to pay it; for he hath no pleasure in fools: pay that which thou hast vowed. Better is it that thou shouldest not vow, than that thou shouldest vow and not pay. Suffer not thy mouth to cause thy flesh to sin ..." (Eccl. 5:4-6).

The prophet is now given the opportunity to fulfil his vow: "And the word of the LORD came unto Jonah the second time, saying, Arise, go unto Nineveh ..." The man who now stands poised to serve God had been brought to an end of himself and to utter dependence on God. In short, he had passed through the experiences of death and resurrection. There can be no better start to service for God than the realisation that we too have passed through death and resurrection: "Know ye not, that so many of us as were baptized into Jesus Christ were baptized into his death? Therefore we are buried with him by baptism into death; that like as Christ was raised up from the dead by the glory of the Father, ***even so we also should walk in newness of life***" (Romans 6:3-4). Paul puts it like this in 2 Corinthians 5 verse 15: "He died for all, that they which live should ***not henceforth live unto themselves, but*** unto him which died for them, and rose again". Previously, Jonah had certainly been living for himself, but now he submits himself to the will of God.

We may divide this Chapter into three sections as follows: ***(1)*** the recommissioning of Jonah (vv.1-4); ***(2)*** the response of Nineveh (vv.5-9); ***(3)*** the repentance of God, (v.10).

1) THE RECOMMISSIONING OF JONAH, vv.1-4

In these verses we should notice the following: ***(a)*** the message to Jonah (vv.1-2); ***(b)*** the obedience of Jonah (v.3); ***(c)*** the preaching of Jonah (v.4).

a) The message to Jonah, vv.1-2

"And the word of the LORD came unto Jonah the second time, saying, Arise, go unto Nineveh, that great city, and preach unto it the preaching that I bid thee." Here are some observations:

i) "The word of the LORD came unto Jonah ***the second time*** ..." (v.1) (The little expression, "the second time", could form the basis of a useful study. See, for example, 1 Kings 19:7.)

Let it be said that it never had to be said of the "greater than Jonas" (Matt.12:41) that "the word of the LORD came ... the second time". Mark particularly presents the Lord Jesus as the Servant of God. It is His actions, rather than His teaching, that Mark emphasises. While Mark, of course, records the Lord's teaching, he does not do so to the extent of the other Gospel writers. One Greek word occurs over forty times in this Gospel and is translated in several ways: "immediately ... straightway ... forthwith ... anon". It is not difficult to imagine the Servant at His work - one task following another. There was no question of a "second time" in the service of the Lord Jesus. He never had to be 'recommissioned'. No wonder the Lord said, "Behold my servant, whom I uphold, mine elect, in whom my soul delighteth" (Isaiah 42:1). The connection between "beloved" and "well pleased" in Matthew 12 verse 18, quoting Isaiah 42 verse 1, harmonises - of course - with the declaration of the Father in Matthew 3 verse 17, "This is my beloved Son, in whom I am well pleased" or "in whom I have found my delight" (JND). This declaration was repeated in Matthew 17 verse 5 when the Lord Jesus was accompanied by Moses and Elijah on the mount of transfiguration. These two men were outstanding servants of God, but only the Lord Jesus could merit unqualified divine approval.

Jonah's previous failure did not disqualify him *ad infinitum* from serving God. The Lord is infinitely gracious and "knoweth our frame; he remembereth that we are dust" (Psalm 103:14). Just think of the way in which the Lord dealt with Peter, and then used him so effectively. Remember too that after previous disappointment, Paul could say of Mark, "Bring him with thee: for he is profitable to me for the ministry". Compare Acts 15 verses 37-39 with 2 Timothy 4 verse 11.

Notice too that God did not recommission Jonah, but decide that in view of past failure on the Nineveh assignment, it would be best to put him on another job! God's original plans are always perfect. Jonah was the best man for the task. Do remember that in God's purposes -

*"There's a work for Jesus none but **you** can do!"*

ii) "Arise, go unto Nineveh, ***that great city*** ..." (v.2). It is also described as ***"an exceeding great city*** of three days' journey" (v.3). J.N.Darby's footnote is rather interesting: "Literally, 'great to God'". Jonah was not asked to undertake a miniscule task for God. It was an immense task, and ***God knew that it was an immense task***. We must never think that service for God is easily accomplished without trouble and difficulty. The size of the task is impressed upon Jonah, but he is assured that God fully understood the situation.

This reminds us that the Lord Jesus was thoroughly aware of the immensity of the task that lay before Him. The Assyrians (Nineveh was their capital city) were noted for their violence and cruelty. The Lord Jesus was fully cognizant of the violence and cruelty which He would endure at the hands of wicked men.

iii) "***Arise, go*** unto Nineveh ... and ***preach unto it the preaching that I bid thee.***" The Lord Jesus, "greater than Jonas", said, "My doctrine is not mine, but his that sent me" (John 7:16); "As my Father hath taught me, I speak these things" (John 8:28); "I speak that which I have seen with my Father" (John 8:38); "For I have not spoken of myself; but the Father which sent me, he gave me a commandment, what I should say, and what I should speak" (John 12:49).

With reference to the command, "Arise, go unto Nineveh ... and preach unto it the preaching that I bid thee", we should notice:

- That the Lord controlled Jonah's ***posture***: "Arise". Sometimes He says, "Come ye yourselves apart into a desert place, and rest a while" (Mark 6:31). Sometimes He says, "Son, go work today in my vineyard" (Matt. 21:28). Here it is, "Arise". Readiness to move when directed. See Luke 1 verse 19.

- That the Lord controlled the ***place*** of Jonah's service: "go unto Nineveh". Let's remember that God has "set the members every one of them in the body, as it hath pleased him" (1 Cor. 12:18). We cannot dictate our position or our service, but we ***are*** to function where God places us.

- That the Lord controlled Jonah's ***preaching:*** "preach unto it the preaching that ***I bid*** thee". Not 'sing unto it' or 'act unto it' but "preach unto it".

So God directs the movements and the message of His servants. We have no right to go where we want to go, and say what we want to say. If you think that is repressive (which you don't, of course), then please remember that obedience to the will of God brings the greatest joy and the greatest liberty.

b) The obedience of Jonah, v.3

"So Jonah arose, and went unto Nineveh, according to the word of the LORD." You don't have to be a genius to construct the little table as follows:

vv.1-2	***v.3***
"The word of the LORD came unto Jonah"	"According to the word of the LORD"
"Arise"	"So Jonah arose"
"Go unto Nineveh"	"And went unto Nineveh"

That's all we really need to say. Christian living is, basically, obedience to God. There's no mystery about it. We do not have to be initiated into some kind of inner circle, or reach some kind of intellectual level. The Lord Jesus said, "If ye love me, keep my commandments" (John 14:15).

c) The preaching of Jonah, v.4

"And Jonah began to enter into the city a day's journey, and he cried, and said, Yet forty days, and Nineveh shall be overthrown." There are at least three things to notice here:

i) Jonah preached without delay. He "began to enter into the city a day's journey, and he cried ..." He didn't wait until the complete journey was finished before preaching. There's no mention of careful and meticulous planning. We can't find any trace of a committee to oversee arrangements, or reference to an 'in depth survey'. He just got on with the job that God had given him to do! That was his only authority. Rather like the newly-saved Saul of Tarsus: "And ***straightway*** he preached Christ in the synagogues, that he is the Son of God" (Acts 9:20). The modern business world abounds with committees. In fact, there often seem to be more committees about work than work itself! An assembly is not a series of committees, but a company of labourers.

Let's face it, had Jonah sat down and weighed up the problems and difficulties that confronted him at Nineveh, he might never have got started! After all, as we have already noted, the Assyrians were a ferocious people, and he was a solitary voice in their vast capital city. If we took time to assess and evaluate the obstacles and opposition in our own localities, we too might be tempted to give it all up as a bad job! If God has called us to serve Him, far better to get on with it.

ii) Jonah preached with earnestness. "And he ***cried.***" There was nothing casual about the preaching. The weight of the message put, to quote the late E.W. Rogers, 'a sufficient gap between his upper and lower dentures!' He didn't mumble – "he cried". It's no good having something important to say if nobody can hear what you're saying!

The need for earnestness was graphically illustrated by C.H. Spurgeon who said that if a man shouted in a weak disinterested voice, 'There's a fire at the back of your house', it was quite likely that the informant would receive the bucket of water! But if he roared ***"F I R E",*** then there must be some urgency! (Kindly supplied by Keith Bintley.)

The earnestness of Jonah must have had a considerable effect on Nineveh. After all, he must rank as the most successful preacher of all time! He knew only too well about the overwhelming judgment of God. He had experienced it himself, and our personal experience of God's dealings makes for very effective preaching.

iii) Jonah preached a solemn message. "Yet forty days, and Nineveh shall be overthrown." (These eight words could well be a summary of his preaching, but this does not in any way cast doubt on the inspiration of the statement: God did not find it necessary to give us any further information.) Not the slightest hint of mercy. Not even a call to repentance. It was all doom and despondency. Jonah was, of course, conveying God's message. It was "the preaching that I bid thee" (v.2). It was "the evil that he had said that he would do unto them" (v.10). How thankful we are that we have an entirely different message. But do let's note nonetheless that Jonah did not shirk the responsibility entrusted to him. He did not evade the fact that God had promised judgment, and we should not evade the fact either.

The 'greater than Jonas' preached a different message (though not devoid of warning: see, for example, Luke 13:1-5): "The Spirit of the Lord is upon me, because he hath anointed me to preach the gospel to the poor; he hath sent me to heal the brokenhearted, to preach deliverance to the captives, and recovering of sight to the blind, to set at liberty them that are bruised, to preach the acceptable year of the Lord" (Luke 4:18-19).

This brings us to the second section of this chapter -

2) THE RESPONSE OF NINEVEH, vv.5-9

"So the people of Nineveh believed God, and proclaimed a fast, and put on sackcloth, from the greatest of them even to the least of them" (v.5). The Lord Jesus referred to their repentance in Matthew 12 verses 39-41. See the Addendum.

The repentance of the Ninevites involved their minds, their bodies and their possessions. Let's look for practical lessons in the passage. After all, "Whatsoever things were written aforetime were written for our learning…" (Rom. 15:4). We must note the following:

i) They "believed God" (v.5). Notice, "believed ***God***". We can legitimately apply the passage to Gospel preaching. When the believers at Thessalonica "received the word of God which ye heard of us, ye received it not as the word of men, but as it is in truth, ***the word of God,*** which effectually worketh also in you that believe" (1 Thess. 2:13). But how about us? That is "us" Christians. Do we always do what the Ninevites did? The behaviour of many Christians and, sadly, the behaviour of many assemblies, strongly suggests that they don't believe the Word of God.

ii) They "proclaimed a fast" (v.5). Nothing else now mattered. Everything else, however legitimate, was put to one side. The mercy and grace of God was all-important. How do we react when the Word of God highlights some area of deficiency, or some sin, in our lives? Anything that brings divine displeasure should be treated as an absolute priority. Paul wrote, "Wherefore we labour ('we are ambitious' or, 'we make it our aim'), that, whether present or absent, we may be accepted ('wellpleasing') of him" (2 Cor. 5:9).

iii) They "put on sackcloth, from the greatest of them even to the least of them" (v.5). In other words, they repented. See verse 8: "Yea, let them turn every one from his evil way, and from the violence that is in their hands". Repentance is seeing sin as God sees it - as something loathsome and disgusting - and turning from it with a sense of horror. It is therefore most solemn that the Lord Jesus had to say "repent" to five out of the seven churches in Revelation 2 & 3.

Since corporate life was at stake, corporate repentance was necessary. It was "from the greatest of them even to the least of them" (v.5). Notice the example of the king of Nineveh. First of all, ***"he arose from his throne" (v.6).*** If we are to please God, there is no question about the occupant of the throne in our life. We too must vacate the throne, and "crown Him Lord of all". Secondly, ***"he laid his robe from him" (v.6).*** All ostentation and pride went. This was no time for finery, pomp or ceremony. He surrendered the dignity of his office. Thirdly, he ***"covered him with sackcloth, and sat in ashes" (v.6).*** He led the nation in mourning and repentance. He was an example of his own edict: "Let neither man nor beast, herd nor flock, taste anything: let them not feed, nor drink water" (v.7). Note his words, "Who can tell if God will turn and repent, and turn away from his fierce anger, that we perish not" (v.9).

This reminds us of the necessity to pray "for kings, and for all that are in authority; that we may lead a quiet and peaceable life in all godliness and honesty" (1 Tim. 2:1-2).

John the Baptist demanded "fruits worthy of repentance". Do notice that it wasn't a case of "sackcloth", and that was all. The "sackcloth" was backed by prayer and action: ***"Cry mightily*** (said the king and his nobles) ***unto God: yea, let them turn every one from his evil way, and from the violence*** (for which Nineveh was noted) ***that is in their hands"*** (v.8). There were to be no 'crocodile tears' in Nineveh.

Even the ***"herd"*** and the ***"flock"*** were involved (v.7). Both "man and ***beast***" were to be covered with sackcloth" (v.8). It seems rather excessive, doesn't it? Until we remember that the "herd" and the "flock" represented the commercial interests of Nineveh. Even this took second place to the overriding necessity to obtain God's mercy. Let's face it, if we let our business interests have precedence in our lives, we cannot expect God's help and blessing. The Lord Jesus said, "Ye cannot serve God and mammon" (Luke 16:13). Getting right with God, and being right with God, involves cost.

Even as Christians, we have sometimes to sing:

Room for pleasure, room for business,
But for Christ the crucified,
Not a place where He can enter
In that heart for which He died.

3) THE REPENTANCE OF GOD, v.10

God spared the Ninevites because they repented, but, sadly, the Lord Jesus had to say of Jerusalem, "How often would I have gathered thy children together, even as a hen gathereth her chickens under her wings, and ye would not! Behold, you house is left unto you desolate ..." (Matt. 23:37-38).

But here, "God saw their works, that they turned from their evil way; and God repented of the evil that he said he would do unto them; and he did it not". There are at least two things to notice here:

i) "God saw their works." It doesn't say, specifically, that 'God heard their prayer'. See verse 8. Undoubtedly, He did hear their prayer, but only because He "saw their works". This is why James tells us that "the effectual fervent prayer of a ***righteous*** man availeth much" (James 5:16). We often quote Psalm 66 in this connection: "Come and hear, all ye that fear God, and I will declare what he hath done for my soul. I cried unto him with my mouth, and he was extolled with my tongue. ***If I regard iniquity in my heart, the Lord will not hear me:*** but verily God hath heard me: he hath attended to the voice of my prayer" (vv.16-19).

ii) "God repented ..." There is hardly any need to say that when applied to God, the word "repent" does not mean sorrow for sin! M.C. Unger puts it rather nicely: "It means to 'relent' in the sense of altering His method of dealing with His creatures since they have changed their ways". God is never inconsistent. When He alters His stated purpose, it is always consistent with His own nature. He "retaineth not his anger for ever, because he ***delighteth in mercy***". Judgment is "his strange work". It is alien to Him. With the change of attitude in Nineveh, God was able to display mercy, instead of the judgment which would have otherwise fallen on the city.

We must remember that in His desire to bless His people, "God is not a man, that he should lie; neither the son of man, that he should repent"

(Num. 23:19). (Note the context.) We must remember too, that "Known unto God are all his works from the beginning of the world ('who does these things known from eternity', JND)" (Acts 15:18). This may partly answer the question, 'Do, or can, our prayers alter the will of God?' While the interface between our prayers and the will of God may not always be easy to discern, we do know that there is a relationship between them – see, for example 2 Corinthians 1 verses 9-11, "But we had the sentence of death in ourselves, that we should not trust in ourselves, but in God which raiseth the dead: who delivered us from so great a death, and doth deliver: in whom we trust that he will yet deliver us; ***ye also helping together by prayer for us*** ..."

What will Jonah do now? Watch this space! But do notice that this chapter ends as it begins: with reference to the grace and mercy of God. God's kindness was extended to Jonah in verse 1, and to Nineveh in verse 10.

ADDENDUM

"The sign of the prophet Jonas", Matthew 12:39

What was the "sign of the prophet Jonas" that brought about repentance at Nineveh? What the Ninevites saw evidently had a salutary effect on the entire city.

The "sign" was evidently the fact that he was "three days and three nights in the whale's belly". The Ninevites knew, presumably, that because of his disobedience, Jonah had been cast into the sea and that normally in such circumstances he would have died. But in it all, he "remembered the LORD" and prayed (2:7).

The lesson was not lost on the men of Nineveh. Jonah had made it clear to them that they were facing divine judgment – "Yet forty days, and Nineveh shall be overthrown" (3:4). But shortly before his arrival in the city, the preacher was himself under judgment, but his evident repentance had led to his deliverance. Would God who had spared the preacher not go further and save them too if they repented? Yes, He would, and He did!

So this generation of Ninevites were 'saved people'? Why not? The Lord Jesus said, "The men of Nineveh shall rise in judgment with this generation, and shall condemn it: because they repented at the preaching of Jonas; and, behold, a greater than Jonas is here (and the 'generation' present when He was here, had ***not*** repented)" (Matt.12:41).

JONAH

6) Read Chapter 4:1-11

Jonah's preaching was incredibly successful. "So the people of Nineveh believed God, and proclaimed a fast, and put on sackcloth, from the greatest of them even to the least of them … and God saw their works, that they turned from their evil way; and God repented of the evil that he had said that he would do unto them; and he did it not" (Jonah 3:5, 10). But the preacher didn't see it like that at all. "It displeased Jonah exceedingly, and he was very angry" (Jonah 4:1).

Centuries later, Peter wrote the following: "The Lord is not slack concerning his promise, as some men count slackness; but is longsuffering to us-ward, not willing that any should perish, but that all should come to repentance" (2 Pet. 3:9). Jonah was the first of two prophets whose sole ministry concerned Nineveh. One hundred and fifty years after Jonah, God used Nahum to pronounce unsparing judgment on the city: "The burden of Nineveh. The book of the vision of Nahum the Elkoshite. God is jealous, and the LORD revengeth; the LORD revengeth, and is furious; the LORD will take vengeance on his adversaries, and he reserveth wrath for his enemies" (Nahum 1:1-2). This time, there was no escape: "The LORD hath given a commandment concerning thee, that no more of thy name be sown … I will make thy grave; for thou art vile" (Nahum 1:14). The book of Nahum certainly proves that "the Lord is not slack concerning his promise". On the other hand, the book of Jonah certainly proves that the Lord "is longsuffering … not willing that any should perish". His mercy extended beyond the boundaries of Israel, and even reached Gentiles in Nineveh. But the prophet didn't learn this lesson very easily. He certainly wasn't in tune with heaven. The Lord Jesus said, "Joy shall be in heaven over one sinner that repenteth" (Luke 15:7).

The Lord Jesus was angry for an entirely different reason. Before He healed the man with "a withered hand" on the sabbath day, before a critical audience, He "looked round about on them with anger, being grieved for the hardness of their hearts …" (Mark 3:1-6).

The book of Jonah ends with a very angry man. God has twice to say to him, "Doest thou well to be angry?" (vv.4, 9). Jonah was angry because God ***spared*** Nineveh, and he was angry because God ***did not spare*** the gourd! With this in mind we may divide the chapter as follows: ***(1)*** Jonah's anger regarding Nineveh (vv.1-4); ***(2)*** Jonah's anger regarding the gourd (vv.5-9); ***(3)*** Jonah's anger rebuked by God (vv.10-11).

1) JONAH'S ANGER REGARDING NINEVEH, vv.1-4

The will of God displeased Jonah, but the Lord Jesus delighted in it. See, for example, Matthew 11 verse 25.

But why was Jonah so angry? He certainly wasn't angry because God had acted out of character. "O Lord, was not this my saying, when I was yet in my country? Therefore I fled before unto Tarshish: for I knew that thou art a gracious God, and merciful, slow to anger, and of great kindness, and repentest thee of the evil" (v.2). (Jonah knew God's character – but still disobeyed Him!) On the contrary, he was angry because God had acted ***in*** character towards people who had no claim whatsoever upon His mercy. It was all so unjust. How could the God of Israel possibly be gracious to people who acted so monstrously towards others?

The prophet was evidently more severe than God Himself - something not entirely unknown elsewhere amongst servants of God. Jonah was happy to preach, "Yet forty days, and Nineveh shall be overthrown". After all, that was what he was told to preach – "preach unto it the preaching that I bid thee". But he was not happy that God was also "gracious … and merciful, slow to anger, and of great kindness". How well do ***we*** know the heart of God? Let's ask the question in two ways:

a) In relation to sinners

Paul reasoned "of righteousness, temperance, and judgment to come" (Acts 24:25). But he also said, "For ***the love of Christ*** constraineth us; because we thus judge, that if one died for all, then were all dead …" (2 Cor. 5:14). The "love of Christ", which held Paul fast, made him an ambassador for Christ. Do our hearts beat in unison with the heart of God with reference to unsaved men and women?

b) In relation to saints

Paul told the Corinthians, "Moreover I call God for a record upon my soul, that to spare you I came not as yet unto Corinth ... I determined this with myself, that I would not come again to you in heaviness ... for out of much affliction and anguish of heart I wrote unto you with many tears" (2 Cor. 1:23 - 2:1-4). Paul did not, for one moment, underestimate the gravity of the problems at Corinth. In fact, he was obliged to say: "What will ye? shall I come unto you with a rod, or in love, and in the spirit of meekness?" (1 Cor. 4:21). The assembly must be a place where divine principles are faithfully maintained, but it must be a place where the saints are "kindly affectioned one to another with brotherly love" (Rom. 12:10). The assembly is not the place where we nurse grievances, or look for opportunity to settle old scores. It is a place where we are "kind one to another, tenderhearted, forgiving one another, even as God for Christ's sake hath forgiven you" (Eph. 4:32).

We sometimes encounter people who delight in taking a 'firm line' and to whom "speaking the truth in love" seems completely alien. How important that our hearts should beat in unison with the heart of God with reference to His people.

But why didn't Jonah think like God? There could be two answers to this:

i) Because his preacher's pride had been injured. This was the man who had said, "Yet forty days, and Nineveh shall be overthrown". But it wasn't overthrown, at least, not in Jonah's lifetime. What about his preaching now? Was Jonah angry because his pride was deeply wounded? Did he put his prowess as a preacher before the best interests of his hearers? Paul wrote to the Philippians, "Look not every man on his own things, but every man also on the things of others" (Phil. 2:4). The Lord Jesus is the greatest example of all in this respect, as Philippians 2 demonstrates. The assembly is not the place where we gratify our personal interests and ambitions, but the place where we seek the interests of our fellow-believers: "Let your moderation (non-insistence on right) be known unto all men" (Phil. 4:5). But perhaps there was another reason for Jonah's anger:

ii) Because he could not reconcile God's mercy on Nineveh with God's love for Israel. The Assyrians, cruel, ferocious and powerful, were a threat to Israel. Had the Ninevites not repented, divine judgment would have engulfed them - which was precisely what Jonah wanted. Assyria would then have been eliminated, and Israel would have been secure. But Jonah knew the character of God: if Nineveh repented, God would be merciful, and Israel would remain under threat. He therefore concluded that it would be in the best interests of God's people not to go to Nineveh in the first place!

But this argument supposes that God's will is not just, and not best. We can be sure that God's will always prove to be just, and always prove to be best. God's purposes are never at variance with themselves. Habakkuk could not understand why God should "raise up the Chaldeans" to chasten His people, when the Chaldeans were infinitely worse than Israel itself! But God made everything very plain to His perplexed servant, who then had to say, "O LORD, I have heard thy speech, and was afraid". Sometimes we have to rest in the will of God, knowing that whilst:

On earth, we have the tears without the reason:
In heaven, we'll have the reason without the tears.

Jonah's prayer ends on a most dejected note: "Therefore now, O LORD, take, I beseech thee, my life from me; ***for it is better for me to die than to live***" (v.3). Rather like Elijah some fifty years before him, "He requested for himself that he might die (but the Lord Jesus ***gave*** His life!); and said, It is enough; now, O LORD, take away my life; for I am not better than my fathers" (1 Kings 19:4). Things hadn't worked out as Jonah desired, and he simply wanted to give it all up! He wouldn't be the last servant of God to give up because he couldn't get his own way! Sometimes we too feel like the Jews in Malachi's day, "It is vain to serve God: and what profit is it that we have kept his ordinances, and that we have walked mournfully before the LORD of hosts?" (Mal. 3:14).

God answered Jonah's prayer with a question, "Doest ***thou*** well to be angry?" The significance of this is quite inescapable. Jonah was angry because God had shewn mercy on Nineveh, quite forgetting that God had also shown to mercy to him! If God had dealt with Jonah, as Jonah wanted God to deal with Nineveh, Jonah would have been dead! Paul said, "I thank Christ Jesus our Lord, who hath enabled me, for that he counted me faithful, putting me into the ministry; who was before a blasphemer, and a persecutor, and injurious: ***but I obtained mercy***" (1 Tim.1:12-13).

It is rather lovely to notice that the very God whose grace and mercy had been questioned by Jonah, now shews grace and mercy to Jonah himself.

Rather than writing off the man as impudent and rebellious, He takes steps to adjust his thinking. So:

2) JONAH'S ANGER REGARDING THE GOURD, vv.5-9

Jonah leaves the sphere of his labours, and waits to see what will happen. "So Jonah went out of the city, and sat on the east side of the city … till he might see what would become of the city." (But the Lord Jesus wept over Jerusalem, Luke 19:41.) It's a very sad situation: Jonah was well aware of God's decision, but he found it quite unacceptable. We must beware: we are all prone to do the same. The New Testament describes a totally different attitude to the Gentiles. You can almost see Jonah looking horrified as Paul talks about "the grace that is given me of God, that I should be the minister of Jesus Christ to the Gentiles, ministering the Gospel of God, that the offering up of the Gentiles might be acceptable, being sanctified by the Holy Ghost" (Rom. 15:15-16). See also verses 8-12. Can you imagine Jonah saying this?! Well, God now prepares three things in order to change Jonah's attitude.

Before we look at the three "prepared" things (to which we should add "the great fish", 1:17), do notice that God is in absolute control of the situation; nothing happens by chance.

a) He "prepared a gourd"

This was, evidently, "the castor oil plant (*palma cristi*), which grows to a height of ten feet with large leaves offering good shade" (M.F. Unger). Jonah was "exceeding glad of the gourd". He valued God's material benefits, and so should we. There is the "gourd" of full employment, the "gourd" of good health, the "gourd" of a nice home, the "gourd" of a happy family … God gives us 'richly all things to enjoy', and we acknowledge that "every good gift and every perfect gift is from above" (James 1:17).

b) He "prepared a worm"

It all happened very quickly – "when the morning rose the next day". All of which reminds us how quickly things can change. The sudden illness … the unexpected redundancy. Just when everything seems set fair for the future … it happens.

c) *He "prepared a vehement east wind"*

Once again, it happened so quickly: "when the sun did arise". Jonah swung quickly from prosperity to adversity and complained bitterly about it: "and the sun beat upon the head of Jonah, that he fainted, and wished in himself to die, and said, It is better for me to die than to live". Let's ponder this for a moment - right out of context!

i) Adversity should never produce bitterness. Paul wrote, "I have learned, in whatsoever state I am, therewith to be content. I know both how to be abased, and I know how to abound: every where and in all things I am instructed both to be full and to be hungry, both to abound and to suffer need. I can do all things through Christ which strengtheneth me" (Phil. 4:11-13). Paul rejoiced in prosperity, and in adversity, but only 'through Christ who pours His strength into me'. True character is revealed more in adversity than in prosperity. The Lord Jesus, when reviled, "reviled not again; when he suffered, he threatened not" (1 Pet. 2:23). Jonah could not understand why his protective gourd should suddenly wither, and complained bitterly about it. He was "exceeding glad for the gourd" (v.6), but became "angry for the gourd" (v.9).

ii) Adversity should produce pleasure for God. "Awake, O north wind; and come thou south; blow upon my garden, that the spices thereof may flow out ..." (Song of Solomon 4:16). The cold north wind, as well as the warm south wind, was necessary to produce fragrance. Beauty of character is so often displayed by saints who are buffeted by the cold winds of adversity and suffering. Their undiminished faith and devotion must bring great pleasure to God.

iii) Adversity introduces us to God's unfailing resources. It was not until "the brook dried up" that Elijah found two things that did not dry up: "the barrel of meal wasted not, neither did the cruse of oil fail" (1 Kings 17:7, 16).

iv) Adversity is intended to promote Christian character. "Ye have forgotten the exhortation which speaketh unto you as unto children, My son, despise not thou the chastening of the Lord, nor faint when thou art rebuked of him." He does this "for our profit, that we might be partakers of his holiness. Now no chastening for the present seemeth to be joyous, but grievous: nevertheless afterward it yieldeth the peaceable fruit of righteousness unto them which are exercised thereby" (Heb. 12:5, 10-12).

God brings into all our lives the "gourd", the "worm", and the "vehement east wind". Sometimes there is 'a shadow over our heads' (v.6). Sometimes, 'the sun beats upon our heads' (v.8).

For the second time, Jonah wanted to die. In the first case, he wanted to die because his personal ambitions had not been achieved. In the second case, he wanted to die because his personal comfort was disturbed. We must now notice the particular lesson for Jonah in all this. It will be a salutary lesson for us too.

3) JONAH'S ANGER REBUKED BY GOD, vv.10-11

The rise and fall of the gourd was deliberately arranged by God. He knew exactly how Jonah would react, and used this to demonstrate his miserable and mean attitude. "Thou hast had pity on the gourd, for the which thou hast not laboured, neither madest it to grow; which came up in a night and perished in a night: ***and should not I spare Nineveh ...?***"

It could be argued that this statement proclaims the sovereignty of God. He is entitled to do as He wishes. See Romans 9 verses 14-24. If He chooses to provide a gourd and then to destroy it: that is His prerogative. If He chooses to have mercy on Nineveh, that, too, is His prerogative. The servant of God must accept the will of God. Whilst the following notes take a different view of the passage, this first explanation is worthy of careful consideration.

i) Jonah was more concerned about a plant than he was about people. He valued a plant more than he valued men. "Thou hast had pity on the gourd." He was much more concerned about one plant than 120,000 people and "much cattle". It could be argued that they were enemies, so why spare them. It's just as well God didn't think about us like that! Read Romans 5 verses 8-10.

ii) Jonah was more concerned about something gratuitously given, than people created and sustained by God. "The gourd, for the which thou hast not laboured, neither madest it to grow." The prophet valued something that cost him nothing, and which had not involved any work or attention on his part. Why then did he fail to understand God's concern about something He had created and on which He had bestowed time and attention?

iii) Jonah was more concerned about something transient, than he

was about people and cattle. "Thou hast had pity on the gourd ... which came up in a night, and perished in a night." The words, "that cannot discern between their right hand and their left hand", probably refer, not to children, but to their complete ignorance of God. How much more the need for mercy! Notice the reference to "much cattle". Perhaps their inclusion with the people of Nineveh indicates both human life, and the support for human life.

We too are surrounded by 'perishables', and we can value them more highly than the souls of men.

O teach me what it meaneth, that cross uplifted high,
With One, the Man of sorrows, condemned to bleed and die.
O teach me what it cost Thee to make a sinner whole,
And teach me, Saviour, teach me, the ***value of a soul.***

This was the lesson that God had to teach Jonah. The Lord Jesus "saw the multitude" and was "moved with compassion on them". A "greater than Jonas" was here. But do we share His compassion?

The book of Jonah ends with a question, and God has not seen fit to record Jonah's response. If He wanted us to know, He would have told us. The important thing is - ***our response.***

MICAH

by

John M Riddle

MICAH

1) INTRODUCTION

"The word of the LORD that came to Micah the Morasthite in the days of Jotham, Ahaz, and Hezekiah, kings of Judah, which he saw concerning Samaria and Jerusalem" (1:1). We should notice five things in connection with the opening verse of the prophecy:

a) The position

Micah was an eighth century prophet, and as we usually say when introducing so-called 'minor prophets' (they were, of course, major men of God), it would be interesting to commence at the exodus from Egypt and construct a complete table of the prophets sent by God. It would begin with Moses (Deut. 18:15; 34:10) and Aaron (Exodus 7:1) and include a great number of men (and some women), some named and some unnamed. The 'writing prophets' alone cover five centuries, viz:

Fifth/sixth century prophets	Haggai, Zechariah, Malachi, Ezekiel, Daniel
Seventh century prophets	Nahum, Habakkuk, Zephaniah, Obadiah, Jeremiah
Eighth century prophets	Hosea, Amos, **Micah**, Isaiah
Ninth century prophets	Jonah, and possibly Joel

The ninth century (801-900 B.C.) brings us to the era of Elijah and Elisha. The tenth century included the unnamed prophet who cried against Jeroboam's altar and the "old prophet in Bethel" (1 Kings 13). David was a prophet: see Acts 2 verse 30. These examples prove that God was not exaggerating when He said, "Since the day that your fathers came forth out of the land of

Egypt unto this day I have even sent unto you all my servants the prophets, ***daily*** rising up early and sending them" (Jer. 7:25). While the oft-quoted words in Acts 14 verse 17 do not refer to the prophets, we can ***apply*** them in that way, and say that God "left not himself without witness" so far as the prophetic testimony was concerned. This should encourage us today: He will continue to maintain testimony to "all the counsel of God" (Acts 20:27), and even when Jerusalem becomes the darkest moral blot on earth, He will give power to His "two witnesses ... these two prophets" (Rev. 11:3-12). When the Lord Jesus was here, people in the city of Nain "glorified God, saying, That a great prophet is risen up among us" (Luke 7:16), but He had to say, "a prophet hath no honour in his own country" (John 4:44).

b) The prophet

"The word of the LORD that came to ***Micah*** the Morasthite." Micah means "Who is like unto Jehovah?", and his name reflected God's character: "Who is a God like unto thee, that pardoneth iniquity, and passeth by the transgression of the remnant of his heritage? he retaineth not his anger for ever, because he delighteth in mercy" (7:18). The ending, Mic***ah***, is an abbreviation of Jehov***ah***. The conduct of some people in the Old Testament totally belied their marvellous names. The sons of Samuel are a case in point: Joel means 'Jehovah is strength', or 'Jehovah is God', and Abiah means 'whose father is Jehovah'. But the conduct of Joel made it abundantly clear that Jehovah was not his God, and the conduct of Abiah made it equally clear that Jehovah was not his father. In view of the fact that James refers to "that worthy name by which ye are called" (James 2:7), we do well to examine our own lives.

c) The place

"Micah the ***Morasthite***." He was from Moresheth. It is called Moresheth-gath (1:14), and was "located about twenty-five miles southwest of Jerusalem near the Philistine border and city of Gath" (*Unger's Commentary on the Old Testament*, p.1847). Gath, Lachish and Adullam were all in the vicinity of his home town. Micah therefore addressed his ***own locality*** in Chapter 1 verses 10-16. According to F.W. Farrar *(The Minor Prophets)*, "The prophet ... takes the names of town after town chiefly in the neighbourhood of his own village". Local men are usually the best people to deal with local conditions, and the ease with which preachers can travel today has not always been beneficial to their local assemblies! Epaphras evidently evangelised his own district: compare Colossians 1 verses 5-7 with Colossians 4 verse 12.

d) The period

"In the days of ***Jotham, Ahaz, and Hezekiah***, kings of Judah." Jotham reigned from 758 B.C. and Hezekiah died circa 697 B.C., which means that Micah lived through changing times. Jotham and Hezekiah were good kings, but Ahaz was exceedingly bad. This therefore makes Micah a contemporary of Isaiah and Hosea. Micah 4 verses 1-3 are an almost exact parallel of Isaiah 2 verses 2-4. But if we charge one of these two prophets with plagiarism, we deny inspiration! Both men "spake as they were moved by the Holy Ghost" (2 Pet. 1:21). Micah 3 verses 12 was cited by some of the elders when Jeremiah was threatened with death for his faithfulness: "Micah the Morasthite prophesied in the days of Hezekiah king of Judah, and spake to all the people of Judah, saying, Thus saith the LORD of hosts, Zion shall be plowed like a field, and Jerusalem shall become heaps, and the mountain of the house as the high places of a forest. Did Hezekiah king of Judah and all Judah put him at all to death? did he not fear the LORD, and besought the LORD, and the LORD repented him of the evil which he had pronounced against them?" (Jer. 26:18-19). Micah's ministry was therefore of great significance in view of Hezekiah's reforms.

e) The prophecy

"The word of the LORD ... which he saw ***concerning Samaria and Jerusalem***." It is addressed to the "whole family" (Amos 3:1), although there is no mention of Samaria after Chapter 1. (Samaria was actually destroyed in Micah's lifetime.) The sections of the prophecy which deal with coming glory of Jerusalem ***omit*** reference to Samaria. ***God does not recognise divisive principles.*** Samaria was a rival system to Jerusalem. God can only bless what is true to His original purpose. This is clear from Galatians 1 verses 6-9, where Paul refers to "another gospel: which is not another", and emphasises the permanence of "that which we preached unto you" and "that ye have received". The original stands! In this connection we should note Romans 16 verse 17, "Now I beseech you, brethren, mark them which cause divisions and offences contrary to the doctrine which ye have learned; and avoid them". However, we ought to carefully ponder the circumstances in which Samaria seceded: see 1 Kings 12.

The prophecy divides into four major sections of similar construction. Each section commences by describing the conditions calling for judgment, and concludes by describing ultimate blessing:

i) ***Dispersion*** and ***Deliverance:*** 1:1 - 2:13

ii) ***Ruin*** and ***Restoration:*** 3:1 - 4:8

iii) ***Travail*** and ***Triumph:*** 4:9 - 5:15

iv) ***Forgetfulness*** and ***Faithfulness:*** 6:1 - 7:20

The basis of divine blessing is not revealed until the final section of the prophecy: see Chapter 7 verses 18-20.

In each of the four sections above which describe Israel's future blessing, Micah refers to the shepherd character of Jehovah:

i) "I will ... put them together as the ***sheep*** of Bozrah, as the ***flock*** in the midst of their fold" (2:12).

ii) "And thou, O tower of the ***flock,*** the stronghold of the daughter of Zion, unto thee shall it come, even the first dominion" (4:8).

iii) "And he shall stand and ***feed*** in the strength of the LORD, in the majesty of the name of the LORD his God" (5:4).

iv) "***Feed*** thy people with thy ***rod***, the ***flock*** of thine heritage, which dwell solitarily in the wood, in the midst of Carmel: let them ***feed*** in Bashan and Gilead, as in the days of old" (7:14).

Each prophecy in 'the book of the twelve' has its own particular characteristics, and the prophecy of Micah emphasises that Jehovah is the "Shepherd of Israel" (Psalm 80:1). It is therefore not without significance that the "ruler in Israel" comes from "Beth-lehem Ephratah", the city of David, the shepherd-king (5:2). He "will come with a strong hand, and his arm shall rule for him: behold, his reward is with him, and his work before him. He shall feed his flock like a shepherd: he shall gather the lambs with his arm, and carry them in his bosom, and shall gently lead those that are with young" (Isaiah 40:10-11). We know Him as "the good shepherd (John 10:11), as "that great shepherd of the sheep" (Heb. 13:20), and as "the chief Shepherd" (1 Pet. 5:4).

We can say of Him, "The Lord is ***my*** shepherd!"

MICAH

2) "The LORD cometh forth out of his place"

Read Chapter 1:1-16

As noted in our introduction, Chapters 1 & 2 represent the first section of the prophecy and can be entitled, 'Dispersion and Deliverance.' For the coming dispersion, see Chapter 1 verse 16 and Chapter 2 verse 10, and for the coming deliverance, see Chapter 2 verses 12-13. Micah introduces his ministry in verse 1, and we should notice the following:

i) He preached nothing but the word of God. "The ***word of the LORD*** that came to Micah the Morasthite in the days of Jotham, Ahaz, and Hezekiah, kings of Judah, which ***he saw*** concerning Samaria and Jerusalem" (v.1). He was unlike the people of whom it was said, "Hear ye indeed, but understand not; and see ye indeed, but perceive not" (Isa. 6:9). The servant of God still needs the faculty of spiritual hearing (see, for example, Rev. 2:7) and the faculty of spiritual sight (Heb. 12:2).

ii) He preached the word of God in changing circumstances. Micah served the Lord during the reigns of two good kings (Jotham and Hezekiah) and one bad king (Ahaz), reminding us that we must "preach the word; be instant ('urgent', JND) in season, out of season" (2 Tim. 4:2). That is, whether it suits people or not.

iii) He preached to a divided nation. His ministry was to both the northern kingdom (Samaria) and the southern kingdom (Jerusalem), highlighting the sad division amongst God's people. Paul censured the divisions in the assembly at Corinth: see 1 Corinthians 1 verses 10-13. Those who sow "discord among brethren" attract divine condemnation. See Proverbs 6 verse 19.

The chapter may be divided as follows: ***(1)*** the executer of judgment (vv.2-4); ***(2)*** the explanation of judgment (v.5); ***(3)*** the execution of judgment (vv.6-16).

1) THE EXECUTER OF JUDGMENT, vv.2-4

"Hear, all ye people; hearken, O earth, and all that therein is: and let the Lord (*Adonahy,* a plural word, meaning 'Sovereign-Lord' or 'Master') GOD (*Jehovah*, the eternal; covenant-keeping God) be witness against you, the Lord *(Adonahy*) from his holy temple" (v.2). While the message was addressed to Samaria and Jerusalem, the whole world was to listen: "Hear all ye people ('peoples', JND); hearken, O earth, and all that therein is". This is emphasised in the translation, 'Hear, ye peoples, ***all of you***; hearken, O earth, and all that is therein' (JND). We should take note of God's dealings with other people. See, for example, Zephaniah 3 verses 6-7 and 1 Timothy 5 verse 20. The words "hear … hearken" stress the necessity to both listen carefully and ***act*** on God's word. How often we listen and do nothing. Notice His omniscience: He is ***aware*** of His people's sin (v.2), and His omnipotence: He ***acts*** against His people's sin (vv.3-4).

i) He is aware of His people's sin, v.2. He is aware of their sin in ***heaven.*** We must notice His perfect knowledge: "Let the Lord GOD be witness against you" (v.2). Compare 2 Chronicles 16 verse 9, "For the eyes of the LORD run to and fro throughout the whole earth". It is still true that "all things are naked and opened unto the eyes of him with whom we have to do" (Heb. 4:13). We must notice His perfect holiness: "the Lord from his ***holy*** temple" (v.2). Compare Habakkuk 2 verse 20, "The LORD is in his holy temple". We must never forget 1 Peter 1 verses 15-16: "As he which hath called you is holy, so be ye holy in all manner of conversation; because it is written, Be ye holy; for I am holy".

ii) He acts against His people's sin, vv.3-4. He acts against their sin on ***earth***. God is not isolated and redundant. He is involved in the affairs of His people. "Behold, the LORD cometh forth out of his place" (v.3). Micah describes the irresistible power with which He intervenes: "And the mountains shall be molten under him, and the valleys shall be cleft, as wax before the fire, and as the waters that are poured down a steep place". According to M.C. Unger, "The images are borrowed from volcanic and earthquake phenomena" and "the heavy rains in Judea in the late fall that cause torrents to gush down the mountains". The language of verses 3-4 recalls Hebrews 12 verse 29, "For our God is a consuming fire". He is completely aware of their condition and will not allow them to continue in sin unchastened and unchecked. Compare 1 Corinthians 3 verse 17, "If any man defile the temple of God, him shall God destroy; for the temple of God is holy, which temple ye are". He will even take away the testimony if it is dishonouring to Him. The assembly at Ephesus was warned that this would happen if there was no repentance and renewal of "the first works" (Rev. 2:5).

2) THE EXPLANATION OF JUDGMENT, v.5

"For the transgression of ***Jacob*** is all this, and for the sins of the house of ***Israel.*** " The two references to the patriarch remind us of God's dealings in sovereign grace with the nation. It has been said that the name 'Jacob' reminds us of the depths to which the grace of God will go to reach a man and that the name 'Israel' reminds us of the heights to which the grace of God will take that same man. But the nation had responded to God's grace with "transgression" and "sin", and in particular the sin of idolatry (v.7).

We should notice that reference is made to the capital cities of the Northern and Southern Kingdoms. "What is the transgression of Jacob? is it not ***Samaria***? And what are the high places of Judah? are they not ***Jerusalem***?" The leadership was held responsible ***then*** (Samaria and Jerusalem were the seats of government), and the leadership is held responsible ***now.*** "A bishop (overseer) must be blameless, as the steward of God" (Titus 1:7). Elders or overseers are not responsible ***to*** the flock, but they are responsible ***for*** the flock. Micah now deals with Samaria and Jerusalem in that order. Who would have thought that Jerusalem, with all its illustrious history, would have been subject to divine judgment? But God does not bless people for 'old times' sake'. See Jeremiah 7 verses 12-15.

3) THE EXECUTION OF JUDGMENT, vv.6-16

Note the progress of the judgment: ***(a)*** it falls on Samaria (vv.6-9); ***(b)*** it approaches Jerusalem (vv.9-16).

a) Judgment falls on Samaria, vv.6-9

i) Her judgment is inevitable, vv.6-7. "Therefore ***I will*** make Samaria as a heap of the field, and as plantings of a vineyard: and ***I will*** pour down the stones thereof into the valley, and ***I will*** discover the foundations thereof" (v.6). Samaria would return to its original state and become a vineyard. "The hill on which Samaria was built was doubtless a vineyard when Omri purchased it from Shema, its original owner" (M.C. Unger). See 1 Kings 16 verse 24. The statement which follows is not easily understood: "And all the graven images thereof shall be beaten to pieces, and all the hires ('harlot-gifts', JND) thereof shall be burned with the fire, and all the idols thereof will I lay desolate: for she gathered it of the hire of a harlot, and they shall return to the hire of a harlot" (v.7). The reference to the destruction of Samaria's idols is clear enough, and "the hires thereof" presumably refers to the gifts offered to the idols. Since idolatry is described as harlotry (see Ezekiel 16:15-16), the gifts offered to idols could be described as "all her harlot-gifts" (JND). If Samaria had become wealthy through gifts offered to idols ("she gathered it of the hire of a harlot"), then her wealth would be carried off by others and offered to their idols: "they (the gifts originally offered to the idols of Samaria) shall return to the hire of a harlot". We know that conquering nations treated the wealth of conquered nations in this way. See, for example, Daniel 1 verse 2.

ii) Her condition is incurable, vv.8-9. See 2 Kings 17 verses 7-18 which fully substantiates the statement, "for her wound is incurable". Compare Jeremiah 30 where similar language is used of Jerusalem ("For thus saith the LORD, Thy bruise is incurable, and thy wound is grievous", v.12), but with promise of recovery ("I will restore health unto thee, and I will heal thee of thy wounds", v.17). There is no promise of recovery for Samaria. It has been suggested that the "wound" refers to the irreversible judgment of God on Samaria rather than to Samaria's incurable sin. In this case, the words which follow, "It is come unto Judah: he ('it', JND) is come unto the gate of my people, even to Jerusalem", must also refer to irreversible judgment, but this was not the case so far as Jerusalem is concerned. The Assyrian first conquered Samaria (2 Kings 17), and then advanced on Jerusalem (2 Kings 18), but retreated in disarray (2 Kings 19). The fact remains that Samaria and Israel came under divine judgment because of refusal to repent: "Yet the LORD testified against Israel, and against Judah, by all the prophets, and by all the seers, saying, Turn ye from your evil ways, and keep my commandments and my statutes, according to all the law which I commanded your fathers, and which I sent unto you by my servants the prophets. Notwithstanding they would not hear, but hardened their necks, like to the neck of their fathers, that did not believe in the LORD their God" (2 Kings 17:13-14). This obliged God to say, "Ephraim is joined to idols: let him alone" (Hos. 4:17).

iii) Her sin is infectious, v.9. "For her wound is incurable; for it is come unto Judah; he is come unto the gate of my people, even to Jerusalem." (***'It*** reacheth unto the gate of my people, even to Jerusalem', JND.) See 2

Kings 17 verse 19, "Also Judah kept not the commandments of the LORD their God, but walked in the statutes of Israel which they made". This recalls the alliances between Samaria and Jerusalem: see, for example, 2 Kings 8 verse 18, "And he (Jehoram, the son of Jehoshaphat) walked in the way of the kings of Israel, as did the house of Ahab: for the daughter of Ahab (Athaliah) was his wife". Compare Ezekiel 23, where Aholah stands for Samaria, and Aholibah stands for Jerusalem. "And Aholah (Samaria) played the harlot when she was mine; and she doted on her lovers, on the Assyrians her neighbours ... And when her sister Aholibah (Jerusalem) saw this, she was more corrupt in her inordinate love than she, and in her whoredoms more than her sister in her whoredoms" (vv.5, 11). We must be careful that ***we*** are not infected by the unscriptural doctrines and practices of Christendom, let alone by the corruption in the secular world. "Wherefore come out from among them, and be ye separate, saith the LORD, and touch not the unclean thing" (2 Cor. 6:17).

Both Samaria and Jerusalem contribute to Micah's personal grief, vv.8-9. "***For this*** (the judgment on Samaria) will I lament, and I will howl ... ***for*** her (Samaria's) wounds are incurable: ***for*** it is come even unto the gate of my people" (vv.8-9 JND). Micah was distressed over the impenitence of Samaria, and the infection of Israel. Paul was distressed as he foresaw the "grievous wolves" from without, and men from within "speaking perverse things" (Acts 20:29-30). We growl and expostulate, but we seldom weep.

b) Judgment approaches Jerusalem, vv.9-16

Disobedience brings the enemy, and results in weakness, defeat, disillusion, captivity and bondage. The enemy is "the rod of mine anger, and the staff in their hand is mine indignation" (Isa. 10:5). These verses do not describe a quirk of fate, for "evil came down from ***the Lord"*** (v.12). Compare Isaiah 45 verse 7, where the words, "I … create ***evil***", meaning sorrow, wretchedness and calamity, refer not to sin, but to "the sure fruits of sin" (C.I. Scofield). This section may well describe the advance of the Assyrian under Sennacherib on Jerusalem eight years later, having conquered Samaria under Shalmaneser. See 2 Kings 18 verses 10, 13-14: "In the sixth year of Hezekiah, that is the ninth year of Hoshea king of Israel, Samaria was taken … Now in the fourteenth year of king Hezekiah did Sennacherib king of Assyria come up against all the fenced cities of Judah, and took them. And Hezekiah king of Judah sent unto the king of Assyria to ***Lachish***".

The towns listed in verses 10-15 lie in south-west Judah, in the plain of Philistia. We should notice the way in which places are specifically mentioned. There is nothing vague about the prophecy. It is not a sweeping generalisation which could mean anything. God's word is always marked by pin-point accuracy. The passage refers to these towns with deep irony: there is evidently a play on their names.

The first place is Gath, a Philistine city. "Gath" sounds like the Hebrew for 'tell'. Being a Philistine city, the words, "Tell it not in Gath", have great significance. The Philistines would have rejoiced that the 'auld enemy' had been successfully invaded. They themselves had successfully invaded part of Judah in the reign of Ahaz. See 2 Chronicles 28 verses 16-19. The enemy delights in the downfall of God's people. We must ensure that, unlike Judah, we give him no opportunity to do so: "give none occasion to the adversary to speak reproachfully" (1 Tim. 5:14).

The play on words continues:

i) "Weep ye not at all", perhaps referring to ***Acco*** (v.10). See JND margin, "In Acco (i.e. 'weeping') weep not". This comes from the Septuagint. According to Unger's Commentary on the Old Testament, the words 'in Accho' sound similar in Hebrew to the word 'weep'. It could be paraphrased, 'Weep not in weep-town'.

ii) "In the house of ***Aphrah*** roll thyself in the dust" (v.10) Aphrah or Beth-le-Aphrah means 'house of dust'. See JND margin. It could be paraphrased, 'Roll in the dust in dust town'.

iii) "Pass ye away, thou inhabitant of ***Saphir,*** having thy shame naked" (v.11). Saphir (JND 'Shaphir') means 'beautiful town'. It could be paraphrased, 'Be in shame in beauty town'.

iv) "The inhabitant of ***Zaanan*** came not forth in the mourning of Beth-ezel" (v.11). Zanaan means 'coming forth'. It could be paraphrased, 'March not forth at march-town.' Unger suggests the paraphrase, 'Stir-town did not stir'. Evidently its inhabitants made no attempt to help the people of nearby Beth-ezel, meaning 'neighbouring house', or 'house nearby'. The words, "He shall receive of you his standing", appear to mean, 'He will take from you its shelter'. There would be no support from Zaanan.

v) "For the inhabitant of ***Maroth*** waited carefully for good; but evil came down from the LORD unto the gate of Jerusalem" (v.12). Maroth means 'bitterness'. It could therefore be paraphrased, 'Evil in bitter-town'.

vi) "O thou inhabitant of ***Lachish,*** bind the chariot to the swift beast" (v.13). We are told that in pronunciation, Lachish sounds like the Hebrew word for team, *'rekesh'*. Hence the rendering, 'Harness the chariot to the team of horses'. It could therefore be paraphrased, 'Bind the chariot to the horse in horse-town'. The words, "She is the beginning of sin to the daughter of Zion: for the transgressions of Israel were found in thee", may refer to the keeping of "the horses that the kings of Judah had given to the sun" (2 Kings 23:11).

vii) "Therefore shalt thou give presents to ***Moresheth-Gath***" (v.14). Moresheth closely approximates to *'morasha'*, meaning a farewell gift, particularly to a bride's dowry. The meaning is obvious: 'Goodbye Morestheth!' Do notice that Micah did not spare his home town. He was consistent. He could not be accused of partiality (1 Tim. 5:21).

viii) "The houses of ***Achzib*** shall be a lie to the kings of Israel" (v.14). Achzib means 'lying'. The name of the city, Hebrew *'akzib'*, becomes *'akzab'*, a failing brook. It could be paraphrased, 'Lies in lie town'. Achzib will not keep back the Assyrian invader.

ix) "Yet will I bring an heir unto thee, O inhabitant of ***Mareshah***" (v.15). Mareshah means possession or inheritance. The heir is the Assyrian invader. It could therefore be paraphrased, 'An heir in inheritance-town'.

x) "He shall come unto ***Adullam*** the glory of Israel" (v.15). Adullam means retreat. It can be rendered, "The glory of Israel (i.e., its nobles) shall come even to Adullam (JND)". The nobility would come like outcasts. See 1 Samuel 22 verses 1-2. It could therefore be paraphrased, 'Retreat to retreat-town'.

The chapter ends with reference to coming captivity: "Make thee bald, and poll thee for thy delicate children; enlarge thy baldness as the eagle; for they are gone into captivity from thee" (v.16). This was expressly forbidden: see Deuteronomy 14 verse 1, "Ye are the children of the LORD your God: ye shall not cut yourselves, nor make any baldness between your eyes for the dead". M.C. Unger quotes B.A. Copass and E.L. Carson *(The Prophet*

Micah): "Perhaps Micah indicated here that Jerusalem is gone so far into heathen practice that even her mourning follows that pattern". All semblance of godliness had gone!

It is an awful thing when the dividing line between the world and the believer disappears. The children of God should never lose their distinctiveness.

MICAH

3) "I will put them together as the sheep of Bozrah"

Read Chapter 2:1-13

This chapter completes the first section of the prophecy and deals in detail with conditions amongst the people of Judah. There are two main chapter divisions: ***(1)*** the reasons for captivity (vv.1-11); (***2)*** the regathering after captivity (vv.12-13).

1) THE REASONS FOR CAPTIVITY, vv.1-11

Two particular reasons are given for the coming captivity anticipated in verse 10, "Arise ye, and depart; for this is not your rest": ***(a)*** they devised evil (vv.1-5); ***(b)*** they deterred the prophets (vv.6-11).

a) They devised evil, vv.1-5

In these verses we must notice ***(i)*** that they devised iniquity against others (vv.1-2); ***(ii)*** that the Lord devised an evil against them (vv.3-5).

i) They devised iniquity against others, vv.1-2

a) They premeditated evil at night, v.1a. "Woe to them that devise iniquity, and work evil upon their beds!" "They lay awake at night planning crooked ways to achieve their selfish schemes" (M.C. Unger). Compare Hosea 7 verses 4-6, "They are all adulterers, as an oven heated by the baker, who ceaseth from raising after he hath kneaded the dough, until it be leavened". This describes an oven whose fire is banked up and needs no immediate attention after fermentation begins. The process proceeds in gentle heat. Hosea continues, "For they have made ready their heart like an oven, whiles they lie in wait: their baker sleepeth all the night; in the morning it burneth as a flaming fire". Some translate, 'all night their anger smoulders'. The night is given to plotting and intrigue, and in the morning, evil is unrestrained.

A different fire burned in the heart of the psalmist: "I was dumb with silence, I held my peace, even from good; and my sorrow was stirred. My heart was hot within me, while I was musing the fire burned: then spake I with my tongue, LORD, make me to know mine end, and the measure of my days, what it is; that I may know how frail I am" (Psalm 39:2-4). He tells us how he spent his waking hours at night. "Stand in awe, and sin not: commune with your own heart upon your bed, and be still" (Psalm 4:4). "My soul shall be satisfied as with marrow and fatness; and my mouth shall praise thee with joyful lips: when I remember thee upon my bed, and meditate on thee in the night watches" (Psalm 63:5-6).

Do we premeditate evil? How can we outsmart or out-manoeuvre another believer in the assembly? How can we achieve or maintain prominence amongst the Lord's people? Selfish ambition and love of place is not unknown amongst the people of God. Far better to seek each other's good. "Let us therefore follow after the things which make for peace, and the things wherewith one may edify another" (Rom. 14:19). After all, love "seeketh not her own, is not easily (RV omits 'easily') provoked, thinketh no evil" (1 Cor. 13:5). There can be righteous anger, but even this must be carefully regulated: see Ephesians 4 verse 26, "Be ye angry, and sin not: let not the sun go down upon your wrath". If we brood on a situation that causes righteous anger, we can so easily overstep the mark, and it becomes sin.

b) They practised evil in the morning, vv.1b-2. "When the morning is light, they practise it, because it is in the power of their hand" (v.1). That is, they had the ability to carry out their predetermined plans. Evil thoughts in the night became evil actions in the day. What we think about is soon evident. Solomon warns against accepting the hospitality of a man with "an evil eye", for this reason: "as he thinketh in his heart, so is he" (Prov. 23:6-7). The Lord Jesus taught that "from within, out of the heart of men, proceed evil thoughts, adulteries, fornications, murders" (Mark 7:21-23). The godly remnant in Malachi's day "feared the Lord, and ... thought upon his name", so we know what they must have talked about when they "spake often one to another" (Mal. 3:16).

The evil practices are named: "They covet fields, and take them by violence; and houses, and take them away: so they oppress a man and his house, even a man and his heritage" (v.2). This was the sin of Ahab: "Give me thy vineyard". To which Naboth replied, "The LORD forbid it me, that I should give the inheritance of my fathers unto thee" (1 Kings 21:1-3). The law said, "Thou shalt not covet thy neighbour's house … nor anything that is thy neighbour's" (Exod. 20:17) and "Thou shalt not remove thy neighbour's landmark, which they of old have set in thine inheritance, which thou shalt inherit in the land that the LORD thy God giveth thee to possess it" (Deut. 19:14). The powerful landowners were intent on total domination. Compare Isaiah 5 verses 8-10, "Woe unto them that join house to house, that lay field to field, till there be no place, that they may be placed alone in the midst of the earth!" Diotrephes had the same spirit: "I wrote unto the church: but Diotrephes, who loveth to have the pre-eminence among them, receiveth us not. Wherefore, if I come, I will remember his deeds which he doeth, prating against us with malicious words: and not content therewith, neither doth he himself receive the brethren, and forbiddeth them that would, and casteth them out of the church" (3 John 9-10). We must beware of a spirit that covets power and influence in the assembly, and which brooks no rival. The Lord Jesus taught that "whosoever will be great among you, shall be your minister: and whosoever of you will be the chiefest, shall be servant of all" (Mark 10:43-44).

ii) The Lord devised an evil against them, vv.3-5

Compare verse 1, "Woe to them that ***devise*** iniquity", with verse 3: "Against this family do I ***devise*** an evil". The lesson is clear: "Be not deceived; God is not mocked: for whatsoever a man soweth, that shall he also reap" (Gal. 6:7). We must notice:

- *The certainty of divine judgment, v.3.* "Therefore thus saith the LORD; Behold, against this family (with all its privileges: see Amos 3:1) do ***I*** devise an evil, from which ye shall ***not remove*** your necks". They might be able to shake off the law, but they would not shake off divine judgment. See 1 Corinthians 3 verses 16-17, "Know ye not that ye are the temple of God, and that the Spirit of God dwelleth in you? If any man defile (mar) the temple of God, him shall God destroy (mar); for the temple of God is holy, which temple ye are". The words, "him shall God destroy", are explained in 1 Corinthians 11 verse 30, "For this cause many are weak and sickly among you, and many sleep".

- *The character of divine judgment, vv.4-5.* They would lose their inheritance. Covetousness leads to emptiness. They would themselves be spoiled and dispossessed. "In that day shall one take up a parable against you, and lament with a doleful lamentation, and say, We be utterly spoiled: he hath changed the portion of my people: how hath he removed it from me! turning away he hath divided our fields" or 'he hath distributed our fields to the rebellious' (JND). The invaders would acquire their fields in exactly the same way as the landowners had illegally acquired property. They would no longer be able to enjoy "the good land which the LORD giveth you" (Deut. 11:17). With the enemy in possession, there would be no requirement for the apportionment of land: "Therefore thou shalt have none that shall cast a cord (a measuring line) by lot in the congregation of the LORD" (v.5). There would be none left with authority to divide the land and place the appropriate landmarks. We have already noticed that the landowners were playing real monopoly in Isaiah 5. But it led to ruin: "In mine ears said the LORD of hosts ('In mine ears Jehovah of hosts hath said', JND), Of a truth many houses shall be desolate, even great and fair, without inhabitant. Yea, ten acres of vineyard shall yield one bath, and the seed of an homer shall yield an ephah" (Isa. 5:9-10).

If we live for ourselves, we will inevitably lose the joy of our inheritance. "There is that scattereth, and yet increaseth: and there is that witholdeth more than is meet, but it tendeth to poverty. The liberal soul shall be made fat: and he that watereth shall be watered also himself" (Prov. 11:24-25). Loss of spiritual enjoyment is an alarm signal that we dare not ignore. This is the lesson of Haggai 1 verses 6-11.

When men are intent on pursuing their own schemes and ambitions, the last thing they want is the word of God. The following verses make this abundantly clear.

b) They deterred the prophets, vv.6-11

In these verses we must notice: ***(i)*** that they rejected the Spirit of God (vv.6-10); ***(ii)*** that they accepted the spirit of falsehood (v.11).

i) They rejected the Spirit of God, vv.6-10

In silencing the prophets, they were silencing the Spirit of God: "Prophesy ye not, say they to them that prophesy: they shall not prophesy to them, that they shall not take shame. O thou that art named the house of Jacob, is the ***Spirit of the LORD*** straitened?" (vv. 6-7). Compare Hosea 9 verse 7, "The prophet is a fool, the spiritual man is mad". The word rendered "prophesy" (it is used again in v.11) means literally, 'to cause to drip or drop' and "lends itself to an unfavourable connotation as 'prate, harp on, utter drivel'" (M.C. Unger). These verses may be understood as follows:

- *The baneful result of silencing the prophets, v.6.* "Prophesy ye not, say they to them that prophesy: ***they shall not prophesy to them, that they shall not take shame***." There are various interpretations, and we should note the following:

"Prophesy ye not, say they to them that prophesy" or "Prophesy ye not, they prophesy" (JND). It can be rendered, literally, 'Don't preach, they preach'. This is clear enough! The verse continues: "They shall not prophesy to them, that they shall not take shame". The AV makes good sense as it stands. They had said, 'Don't preach!': very well, the prophets will do as they are told, and that meant that the covetous wealthy men would never be troubled by their consciences. After all, these nasty prophets had a terrible knack of awakening the conscience! In other words, in silencing the prophets, they silenced their own consciences. JND renders this part of the verse as follows: "Prophesy ye not, they prophesy. If they do not prophesy to these, the ignominy will not depart". That is, if the prophets were silenced, there would be no salvation from the situation. The matter would never be dealt with. Alternatively, it could be rendered, "One should not preach of such things; disgrace will ***not*** overtake us" (RSV). That is, the prophets were to be silenced, because it was quite unthinkable that Israel would be dispossessed of their national inheritance. They would never go into captivity!

But whichever way the original text is rendered, one thing is clear: only the word of God could redress the situation, but that is precisely what they ***did not want to hear!*** Micah was by no means alone in facing this situation. See Amos 7 verses 10-13, Jeremiah 11 verses 18-23, 26 verses 10-24.

- *The beneficial result of hearing the prophets, v.7.* "O thou that art named the house of Jacob, is the spirit of the LORD straitened? Are these his doings? Do not my words do good to him that walketh uprightly?" We should notice the expression, "house of Jacob": it emphasises the depths of divine grace.

The first two questions emphasise that blame for the coming captivity could not be assigned to God. It was not His will that His people should be afflicted in this way. *The Pulpit Commentary* puts it like this: "'Is the spirit of the LORD straitened?': that is, when His judgments overtake men for their sins, is this to be regarded as a token that God's loving-kindness and long-suffering have failed? No: His compassions never fail. 'Are these his doings?': that is, is God the author and cause of the evils men have to experience when they stray from righteousness? No, He cannot be; these are to be traced to the wrong-doers themselves". Compare Isaiah 50 verse 1, "Thus saith the LORD, Where is the bill of your mother's divorcement, whom I have put away? or which of my creditors is it to whom I have sold you? Behold, for your iniquities have ye sold yourselves, and for your transgressions is your mother put away".

The third question is telling in the extreme: "Do not my words do good to him that walketh uprightly?" God always has in mind the blessing of His people through His word. All who walk uprightly have nothing to fear from the word of God. The very fact that they were saying, 'Preach not', was evidence that they were ***not walking uprightly.*** The believer who desires to walk with God need never be afraid of exposing himself to God's word. God's word may "do good" by causing us spiritual discomfort, or it may "do good" by causing spiritual joy, but it will ***always*** "do good". The spiritual man rejoices in the truth: the unspiritual man desires anything but the truth! "He that ***hath an ear***, let him hear."

But God's people were not walking uprightly. They were treating their brethren as an enemy would treat them. "Even of late my people is risen up as an enemy" (vv.8-9). It is tragic when relationships between God's people sink to the level of relationships between the unregenerate, and sometimes even lower. Paul was obliged to charge the Galatians with spiritual cannibalism. See Galatians 5 verse 15. The bitterness and acrimony that sometimes exists between believers is an utter disgrace. These verses describe two classes of oppressed people.

- *The unsuspecting, v.8.* "Ye pull off the robe with the garment from them that pass by securely as men averse from war", or "Ye strip off the mantle with the garment from them that pass by securely, that are averse from war" (JND). That is, from those that pass by trustingly, with no thought of war. Compare Exodus 22 verses 26-27, "If thou at all take thy neighbour's raiment to pledge, thou shalt deliver it unto him by that the sun goeth down".

- *The unresisting, v.9*. "The women of my people have ye cast out from their pleasant houses; from their children have ye taken away my glory for ever." 'The second example was another glaring example of Israel's rejection of the word of God in the plunder of unsuspecting and helpless society, involving oppression of the widow and the orphan' (M.C. Unger). The expression, "their pleasant houses", is, literally, 'house of delights': that is, the widow's home, which has been her delight. See Unger again: 'The food, clothing, and shelter of those helpless members of society, which had been given them as the result of God's blessing upon them, and thus reflected God's 'glory', had been removed "forever" by those rejecters of God's word, indicating no sense of repentance but, rather, steadfast persistence in their sin'. These people had their counterparts in the New Testament. "Woe unto you, scribes and Pharisees, hypocrites! for ye devour widows' houses, and for a pretence make long prayer: therefore ye shall receive the greater damnation" (Matt. 23:14).

Their covetousness damaged others. We can be guilty too, if not in the same way, then certainly by neglect. We must be careful how we treat each other. Our brethren are God's people. A trespass against a brother was a trespass against God. See Leviticus 6 verses 1-7. Notice Luke 15 verse 20: "Father, I have sinned against ***heaven***, and in thy sight". We must carefully note the teaching of the New Testament. See 1 Corinthians 12 verse 25, "There should be no schism in the body; but that the members should have the same care one for another"; Ephesians 4 verse 32, "Be ye kind one to another, tenderhearted, forgiving one another, even as God for Christ's sake hath forgiven you"; 1 John 3 verse 17, "But whoso hath this world's good, and seeth his brother have need, and shutteth up his bowels of compassion from him, how dwelleth the love of God in him?" See also James 2 verses 15-16.

The treatment of God's people in this way would result in dispossession: "Arise ye, and ***depart***; for this is not ***your rest*** (but it will be in the future: see Isaiah 11:10): because it is polluted, it shall destroy you, even with a sore destruction" (v.10). Compare Leviticus 18 verse 28: God's people were to keep His statutes and judgments "that the land spue not you out also, when ye defile it, as it spued out the nations that were before you". Those who had cast out women and children from their homes would themselves be cast out of the land.

ii) They accepted the spirit of falsehood, v.11

If men reject the truth, they are vulnerable to lies. See 2 Thessalonians 2 verses 11-12, "And for this cause God shall send them strong delusion, that they should believe a lie: that they might all be damned who believed not the truth, but had pleasure in unrighteousness". Micah proceeds: "If a man, walking in the spirit and falsehood do lie, saying, I will prophesy unto thee of wine and of strong drink; he shall even be the prophet of this people". This does not mean that the man was drunk, but that he predicted carnal pleasure and all that was associated with it. "He would flatter their wishes, and pander to their lusts" (M.C. Unger). No doubt he had a very full diary! In accepting the false prophet, they were accepting the spirit of falsehood. Compare 2 Timothy 4 verses 3-4, "For the time will come when they will not endure sound doctrine; but after their own lusts shall they heap to themselves teachers, having itching ears; and they shall turn away their ears from the truth, and shall be turned unto fables". People do like to hear what they like to hear! It is significant that the false prophets never predicted divine wrath. In Jeremiah's day, they predicted the raising of the Chaldean siege, the return of the temple treasures, but never divine judgment. They were very popular! That was exactly what the people wanted to hear! But now the subject matter in the chapter changes, and our attention is drawn to events at the end-time.

2) THE REGATHERING AFTER CAPTIVITY, vv.12-13

The divine Shepherd will regather His flock. "***I will*** surely assemble, O Jacob, all of thee; ***I will*** surely gather the remnant of Israel; ***I will*** put them together as the sheep of Bozrah (meaning 'sheepfold' and located in Edom), as the flock in the midst of their fold: they shall make great noise by reason of the multitude of men (possibly referring to their cries in captivity: compare Exodus 3:7-8). The breaker is come up before them (JND, 'One that breaketh through is gone up before them'); they have broken up (i.e. broken out of captivity), and have passed through the gate, and are gone out by it; and their king (David: see Ezek. 34:23-24) shall pass before them, and the LORD on the head of them." It is to this "remnant" (v.12) that Paul refers in Romans 11 verse 26, "And so all Israel shall be saved: as it is written, There shall come out of Sion the Deliverer, and shall turn away ungodliness from Jacob". The promise of scattering ("Arise ye, and depart", v.10), must be compared with the promise of regathering ("I will surely assemble, O Jacob, all of thee", v.12). God did not intend to leave His people in perpetual captivity. This is the first of a series of references to the shepherd-character of Jehovah. (See 4:8, 5:2, 5:4, 5:5, and 7:14.) When the Lord regathers His flock, their Shepherd-King will be "great unto the ends of the earth" (5:4).

MICAH

4) "I am full of power by the spirit of the LORD"

Read Chapter 3:1-12

In our introductory study we suggested that Chapters 1 & 2 can be entitled ***'Dispersion and Deliverance'*** ("For they are gone into captivity from thee", 1:16; "The breaker is come up before them", 2:13), and that Chapters 3 verse 1 – 4 verse 8, the second section of the prophecy, can be entitled ***'Ruin and Restoration'***. For coming ruin, see Chapter 3 verse 12, "Therefore shall Zion for your sake be plowed as a field", and for coming restoration, see Chapter 4 verse 8, "The kingdom shall come to the daughter of Jerusalem".

This part of the prophecy follows the general pattern of each section in which God first gives reasons for judgment on the nation, and then reveals His ultimate mercy to them. Chapter 3, therefore, gives the contributory factors to national disaster. They are summarised in verse 11, "The ***heads*** thereof judge ***for reward***, and the ***priests*** thereof teach ***for hire***, and the ***prophets*** thereof divine ***for money***". These people represent the national leadership, with responsibility for judgment and equity, and for guidance and instruction. Three classes of people are singled out for divine comment: ***(i)*** the princes (or "heads"), ***(ii)*** the priests and ***(iii)*** the prophets. All three classes are charged with a preference for money rather than for truth. It was a time of bribery and corruption.

The apostle Paul had a clear conscience in the matter: "For we are not as many, which corrupt (make a trade) the word of God: but as of sincerity, but as of God, in the sight of God speak we in Christ" (2 Cor. 2:17). He continues, "But have renounced the hidden things of dishonesty (or 'shame', referring to the preceding quotation), not walking in craftiness, nor handling the word of God deceitfully; but by manifestation of the truth commending ourselves to every man's conscience in the sight of God" (2

Cor. 4:2). See also 1 Thessalonians 2 verses 3-6: "For our exhortation was not of deceit, nor of uncleanness, nor in guile. But as we were allowed of God to be put in trust with the gospel, even so we speak; not as pleasing men, but God, which trieth our hearts. For neither at any time used we flattering words, as ye know, nor a cloak of covetousness; God is witness: nor of men sought we glory, neither of you, nor yet of others, when we might have been burdensome as the apostles of Christ". Compare 1 Corinthians 9. There must be purity of motive and faithfulness to the word of God in all our service for Him.

There are two major sections in the chapter, each introduced by, "Hear, I pray you, O ***heads*** of Jacob, and ye ***princes*** of the house of Israel" (vv.1, 9). Attention is drawn ***(1)*** to the flagrant conduct of the leadership (vv.1-8) and ***(2)*** to the false confidence of the leadership (vv.9-12). We should notice that Micah begins by saying "And ***I*** said, Hear, ***I*** pray you (v.1), but continues by saying, "Thus saith the ***LORD***" (v.5). Compare 2 Chronicles 36 verses 21-22 which refer to: "the word of the LORD by the mouth of Jeremiah".

1) THE FLAGRANT CONDUCT OF THE LEADERSHIP, vv.1-8

This section deals with two of the three classes noted above: ***(a)*** the princes (vv.1-4); ***(b)*** the prophets (vv.5-8).

a) The princes, vv.1-4

These were men responsible for implementing justice and exercising care for the nation. They were to rule for God. But Micah 3 verses 1-3 make clear that there was no care and no judgment: rather, oppression and suppression: "And I said, Hear, I pray you, O heads of Jacob, and ye princes of the house of Israel; Is it not for you to know judgment? Who hate the good and love the evil; who pluck off their skin from off them, and their flesh from off their bones; who also eat the flesh of my people, and flay their skin from off them; and they break their bones, and chop them in pieces, as for the pot, and as flesh within the caldron". Whilst this refers particularly to the leadership, we must all avoid treating each other in this way. See Galatians 5 verse 15 and James 4 verses 1-2. We can easily damage God's people by unwarranted criticism and intemperate language.

They would be unheard by God when calamity comes: "Then they shall cry unto the LORD, but he will not hear them: he will even hide his face from them at that time, as they have behaved themselves ill in their doings" (v. 4). As with the prophets in verse 7, there would be "no answer of God".

Care for the people of God is most important and must not be influenced by bias or preference. Responsible brethren may not be influenced by money, but they can be influenced by other even more subtle influences! It is not without significance that we learn in Colossians 4 verse 10 that John Mark was "sister's son to Barnabas". Perhaps his decision in Acts 15 verse 37 was influenced by family considerations. Caring men will recognise their responsibility to ***God***. An elder is a ***shepherd*** to the flock, but he is a ***steward*** to God: see Titus 1 verse 7, "for a bishop must be blameless, as the steward of God". He is responsible to God in connection with "the church of ***God***". Hence Acts 20 verse 28, "Take heed therefore unto yourselves, and to all the flock ... which he hath purchased with his own blood (the blood of his own)". We should notice some New Testament words in this connection:

a) Ruling. See Romans 12 verse 8, "He that ruleth, with diligence ('earnestness' or 'zeal')". The Greek word *(proistemi)* means 'to stand before'. See also 1 Timothy 5 verse 17. A different word is employed in Hebrews 13: "Remember them which have the rule over you ... Obey them that have the rule over you ... Salute all them that have the rule over you" (vv. 7, 17, 24). Here the Greek word *('hegeomai')* means 'to lead'. Hence the New Translation (JND), "Remember your ***leaders*** ... Obey your ***leaders*** ... Salute all your ***leaders"***. Elders must be seen and heard, not as despots, but as spiritual guides. After all, a shepherd leads and speaks!

b) Tending. This is the meaning of the word rendered "feed" in a number of AV passages. See, for example, Acts 20 verse 28, "Take heed therefore unto yourselves, and to all the flock, over (in) the which the Holy Ghost hath made you overseers, to ***feed*** (JND 'shepherd') the church of God". It is more than feeding: it covers the whole range of shepherd-care. See 1 Timothy 3 verse 5, "take care of the church of God", where the expression "take care" must be understood with reference to Luke 10 verses 34-35.

c) Overseeing. Its meaning can be understood very clearly by the expression ***"looking diligently"*** (Heb. 12:15). The same Greek word is rendered ***"oversight"*** in 1 Peter 5 verse 2. Significantly, a later form of the Greek word is used in the New Testament in connection with visiting! See, for example,

James 1 verse 27, “Pure religion and undefiled before God and the Father is this, To ***visit*** the fatherless and widows in their affliction”.

b) The prophets, vv.5-8

These were the men with responsibility for communicating the word of God. The preaching men. Micah describes two classes of prophets here:

i) The prophets without the word of God, vv.5-7

“Thus saith the LORD concerning the prophets that make my people err, that bite with their teeth, and cry, Peace; and he that putteth not into their mouths, they even prepare war against him” (v.5). We should notice:

- Their message. The prophets, divining for men, were giving their patrons ***what they wanted to hear!*** Their message was “Peace!” (See also Jer. 6:14; 8:11, “They have healed also the hurt of the daughter of my people slightly, saying, Peace, peace: when there is no peace”.) Compare Micah 2 verse 11, “If a man walking in the spirit (JND, ‘wind’) and falsehood do lie, saying, I will prophesy unto thee of wine and strong drink; he shall even be ***the prophet of this people***”. This is updated in 2 Timothy 4 verse 3, “For the time will come when they will not endure the sound doctrine; but, having itching ears, will heap to themselves teachers after their own lusts” (RV). It is all too easy to follow the false prophets, and ‘play to the gallery!’ Our business is to “preach the word; be instant (urgent) in season, out of season” (2 Tim. 4:2). We must do this in all circumstances, whether favourable or otherwise (“in season, out of season”). There will be no peace for Israel until the Shepherd-King reigns: He “shall be the peace” (Micah 5:5).

- Their motive. This is abundantly clear: “And he that putteth not into their mouths, they even prepare war against him”.

As noted previously, the times were marked by the repression of true prophecy, see Chapter 2 verses 6-7, and the encouragement of false prophecy, see Chapter 2 verse 11. But the false prophets had nothing to say, and there was no answer from God. “Therefore night shall be unto you, that ye shall not have a vision: and it shall be dark unto you, that ye shall not divine; and the sun shall go down over the prophets, and the day shall be dark over them. Then shall the seers be ashamed, and the diviners confounded: yea, they shall all cover their lips (like the leper, Lev. 13:45);

for there is no answer of God" (vv.6-7). By covering their lips the prophets are admitting that they now have nothing to say.

ii) The prophet with the word of God, v.8

Against this dark background, Micah, the true prophet, stood in sharp contrast: "But truly I am full of power by the spirit of the LORD, and of judgment, and of might, to declare unto Jacob his transgression, and to Israel his sin". The chilling words, "There is no answer from God", did not apply to him! He did not have to cover his lips! He was fearless in preaching, and we do well to emulate him. In Gospel preaching, it is our business to "preach the word"; or in teaching, it is our business to declare "all the counsel of God".

The false prophets were under the ***power of money***: they pleased ***their patrons***. They did ***not*** declare "unto Jacob his transgression, and to Israel his sin". Micah was under the ***power of the Spirit:*** he pleased ***the Lord.*** In a day when the cry was, "Is not the LORD among ***us***?" (v.11) the Lord was with ***Micah***. He enjoyed the ***reality*** of God's presence, to which Israel only paid lip-service.

The only resource in days of declension and decline is the power of God's gracious Spirit. See Zechariah 4 verse 6; 1 Corinthians 2 verse 4: the false prophets used "enticing words of man's wisdom", but Micah spoke "in demonstration of the Spirit and of power". It is important to remember that while in the Old Testament, the presence and power of the Holy Spirit was experienced by servants of God on particular occasions and for limited periods (see, for example, Judges 3:10, 6:34, 14:6), He now indwells each believer permanently. See John 14 verse 16. The words, "But truly I am full of power by the spirit of the LORD", remind us of New Testament teaching. The expression, "filled with the Spirit", occurs fifteen times in the New Testament: four times in Luke, ten times in Acts, and once in the epistles (Eph. 5:18). The references subdivide into two sections: ***the first signifying a sovereign act***, and ***the second signifying the normal tenor of life***. The Holy Spirit gives us particular help for special occasions, as well as the help we need for everyday life.

- *A sovereign act*. The Greek word *pletho* is used in this connection. See Wigram's concordance: Luke 1 verse 15, "He (John) shall be ***filled*** with the Holy Ghost"; Luke 1 verse 41, "Elisabeth was ***filled*** with the Holy Ghost"; Luke 1 verse 67, "His father Zacharias was ***filled*** with the Holy Ghost"; Acts

2 verse 4, "They were all ***filled*** with the Holy Ghost"; Acts 4 verse 8, "Then Peter, ***filled*** with the Holy Ghost"; Acts 4 verses 31-33, "They were all ***filled*** with the Holy Spirit, and they spake the word of God ***with boldness*** ... and with great power gave the apostles witness of ***the resurrection of the Lord Jesus"***; Acts 9 verse 17, "That thou mightest receive thy sight, and be ***filled*** with the Holy Ghost"; Acts 13 verse 9, "Saul ... ***filled*** with the Holy Ghost".

We conclude that the word employed by the Holy Spirit in these cases signifies a sovereign act by God in giving special help in special circumstances. Two cases evidently refer to the initial reception of the Holy Spirit (Luke 1:15 and Acts 9:17). In Acts, the ***act*** of being "filled with the Holy Ghost" refers to two groups and three individual cases.

- ***Normal tenor of life***. The Greek word *pleroo*, or its past tense form, is employed in this connection. The word signifies what the Lord Jesus, the seven "deacons", Stephen and Barnabas and others were ***customarily.*** See Luke 4 verse 1, "And Jesus (omit 'being') ***full*** of the Holy Ghost"; Acts 6 verse 3, "Men ... ***full*** of the Holy Ghost and wisdom"; Acts 6 verse 5, "A man ***full*** of faith and of the Holy Ghost"; Acts 7 verse 55, "But he, being ***full*** of the Holy Ghost, looked up steadfastly into heaven, and saw the glory of God, and Jesus standing on the right hand of God"; Acts 11 verse 24, "For he was a good man, and ***full*** of the Holy Ghost and of faith"; Acts 13 verse 52, "And the disciples were ***filled*** with joy, and with the Holy Ghost"; Ephesians 5 verse 18, "And be not drunk with wine, wherein is excess; but be ***filled*** with the Spirit". These references describe the constant state of being "filled with the Holy Ghost". Ephesians 5 verse 18 is an exhortation: it does not describe a sovereign act.

2) THE FALSE CONFIDENCE OF THE LEADERSHIP, vv.9-12

They said, ***"Is not the LORD among us? none evil can come upon us"*** (v.11). As on other occasions, this was mere lip-service. See Matthew 15 verse 8, citing Isaiah 29 verse 13, "This people draweth nigh unto me with their mouth, and honoureth me with their lips; but their heart is far from me". The leadership falsely claimed to "lean upon the LORD" (v.11) but in the 'upper room', John leant "on Jesus' bosom" (John 13:23).

The section is introduced by the words, "Hear this, I pray you, ye heads of the house of Jacob, and princes of the house of Israel". This section deals with three classes, all of which are charged with the same sin of covetousness.

a) The princes, vv.9-11

"Hear this, I pray you, ye heads of the house of Jacob, and princes of the house of Israel, that abhor judgment, and pervert all equity. They build up Zion with blood, and Jerusalem with iniquity. The heads thereof judge ***for reward***." It was a far cry from 2 Chronicles 19 verses 6-9, where Jehoshaphat "said to the judges, Take heed what ye do: for ye judge ***not for man***, but ***for the LORD***, who is with you in the judgment. Wherefore now let the fear of the LORD be upon you; take heed and do it: for there is no inquity with the LORD our God, nor respect of persons, nor taking of gifts ... and he charged them, saying, Thus shall ye do in the fear of the LORD, faithfully, and with a perfect heart". Compare Ezekiel 34 verse 2, "Woe be to the shepherds of Israel that do feed themselves! should not the shepherds feed the flocks?"

b) The priests, v.11

"The priests thereof teach ***for hire***." The priesthood is censured in Malachi 2, with the observation, "For the priest's lips should keep knowledge, and they should seek the law at his mouth: for he is the messenger of the LORD of hosts" (v.7). See Leviticus 10 verses 9-11 and 2 Chronicles 15 verse 3. God's people were to be instructed by priestly men. We can only help God's people if we are in touch with ***God Himself***, and we can only help God's people if we are in touch with the ***word of God.***

c) The prophets, v.11

"The prophets thereof divine ***for money.***" See verse 5, "He that putteth not into their mouths, they even prepare war against him". Paul was able to tell the Ephesians elders that he had "coveted no man's silver, or gold, or apparel", and continued by saying, "These hands have ministered unto my necessities, and to them that were with me" (Acts 20:33-34).

But the ***crowning sin*** was this: "Yet will they (i.e. the heads ... priests ... prophets) lean upon the LORD, and say, Is not the LORD among us? none evil can come upon us" (v.11). ***They associated the Lord with their malpractices.*** Compare Jeremiah 7 verses 4-10. "Trust ye not in lying words, saying, The temple of the LORD, The temple of the LORD, The temple of the LORD, are these (JND, 'is this') ... Will ye steal, murder, and commit adultery, and swear falsely, and burn incense unto Baal, and walk after other gods whom ye know not; and come and stand before me in this house, which is called by my name, and say, We are delivered to do all these abominations?" See also 1 Samuel 4 verse 3, "Let us fetch the ark of the covenant of the LORD out of Shiloh unto us, that, when ***it*** cometh among us, ***it*** may save us out of the hands of our enemies". They were using the ark as a 'lucky mascot.' They were like Samson who "wist not that the LORD was departed from him" (Judges 16:20).

Where there is no spiritual rule and care, no true priesthood, and no declaration of the mind of God, we cannot expect the Lord's presence and preservation, but only ***destruction and desolation.*** Hence, "***Therefore*** shall Zion for your (i.e. the princes, priests, and prophets) sake be plowed as a field, and Jerusalem shall become heaps, and the mountain of the house as the high places of the forest" (v.12). Let every assembly be warned! When the life of Jeremiah was threatened by "the priests and the prophets", the people were reminded of the way in which Hezekiah responded to this very verse: "Micah the Morasthite prophesied in the days of Hezekiah king of Judah, and spake to all the people of Judah, saying, Thus saith the LORD of hosts, Zion shall be plowed like a field, and Jerusalem shall become heaps, and the mountain of the house as the high places of a forest. Did Hezekiah king of Judah and all Judah put him at all to death? did he not fear the LORD, and besought the LORD, and the LORD repented him of the evil that he pronounced against them? Thus might we procure great evil against our souls" (Jer. 26:11, 18-19). This certainly confirms that Micah was not exaggerating when he said that he declared "unto Jacob his transgression, and to Israel his sin" (v.8). The presence of the king did not deter him. He was faithful before great and small.

Chapter 3 therefore closes with Jerusalem ***ruined*** because the word of God had been rejected in favour of material profit. "Therefore shall Zion for your sake be plowed as a field, and Jerusalem shall become heaps, and the mountain of the house as the high places of the forest" (v.12). Chapter 4 commences with ***restoration***. "But in the last days it shall come to pass, that the mountain of the house of the LORD shall be established in the top of the mountains" (v.1).

MICAH

5) "Let us go up to the mountain of the LORD"

Read Chapter 4:1-8

Micah Chapter 3 ends with ***ruin:*** "Therefore shall Zion for your sake be plowed as a field, and Jerusalem shall become heaps, and the mountain of the house as the high places of the forest" (v.12). Chapter 4 commences with ***restoration:*** "But in the last days it shall come to pass, that the mountain of the house of the LORD shall be exalted in the top of the mountains" (v.1). Notice that in Chapter 3 verse 12 it is the "mountain of the house", whereas in Chapter 4 verse 1 it is called "the mountain of the house ***of the LORD***". We may divide the passage as follows: ***(1)*** the supremacy of the kingdom (vv.1-3); ***(2)*** the security of the kingdom (vv.4-5); ***(3)*** the strength of the kingdom (vv.6-8).

1) THE SUPREMACY OF THE KINGDOM, vv.1-3

The first and last verses of the passage (note the parallel verse in Isaiah 2 verse 2 which is followed by an appeal to the nation in Isaiah's lifetime, v.5) stress the supremacy of Israel in the last days. "But in the last days it shall come to pass, that the mountain of the house of the LORD shall be exalted in the top of the mountains, and it shall be exalted above all hills; and people shall flow unto it" (v.1). Compare verse 8, "And thou, O tower of the flock, the strong hold of the daughter of Zion, unto thee shall it come, ***even the first dominion***; the kingdom shall come to the daughter of Jerusalem". "The mountain of the house of the LORD" will not be mount Moriah, but a new elevation. Ezekiel describes an area, 25,000 cubits square, lying between the territory of Judah and Benjamin: "and the sanctuary shall be in the midst of it" (Ezek. 48:8).

At the time of the tribulation, God "will gather all nations against Jerusalem to battle; and the city shall be taken" (Zech. 14:2). The city is yet to fall again in battle, but only to be rebuilt for a thousand years of undisturbed peace and security. The glory of the city, with its temple and environs, is described in Ezekiel 40-48. Isaiah 62 is devoted to the coming glory of the city. The chapter commences, "For Zion's sake will I not hold my peace, and for Jerusalem's sake I will not rest, until the righteousness thereof go forth as brightness, and the salvation thereof as a lamp that burneth" (v.1). It ends, "And they shall call them, The holy people, The redeemed of the LORD: and thou shalt be called, Sought out, A city not forsaken" (v.12). We should note the following:

a) Its spiritual position, v.1

Notice that it is not called, initially, "Zion" or "Jerusalem", but "the mountain of the ***house of the LORD"***. See Ezekiel 48 verse 35: "And the name of the city from that day shall be, ***The LORD is there***". It will be recognised as "the city of the great King" (Psalm 48:2). God will say, "Yet have I set my king upon my holy hill of Zion" (Psalm 2:6). It will then be said, "Cry out and shout, thou inhabitant of Zion: for great is the Holy One of Israel in the midst of thee" (Isaiah 12:6). This will be the city over which the Lord Jesus once wept, "Saying, If thou hadst known, even thou, at least in this thy day, the things which belong unto thy peace!" (Luke 19:42).

The assembly should be similarly recognised. Every assembly should covet the words of Mark 2 verse 1, "It was noised that he was in the house". Paul explained the effect of godly order on visitors to the assembly, as follows: "So falling down on his face he will worship God, and report that God is in you of a truth" (1 Cor. 14:25).

b) Its geographical position, v.1

"But in the last days it shall come to pass, that the mountain of the house of the LORD shall be established in ***the top of the mountains***, and it shall be exalted ***above the hills***." Its physical elevation will answer to its spiritual elevation. Zechariah 14 describes the geographical and geological changes that will take place to make this possible. At present, Jerusalem is ***not*** "established in the top of the mountains", but that will change when Messiah returns to the mount of Olives. The mountain will then "cleave in the midst thereof toward the east and toward the west, and there shall be a very great valley; and half of the mountain shall remove toward the north, and half of it toward the south" (Zech. 14:4). Two rivers will flow along the newly created valleys: one will flow ***east*** to the Dead Sea, and the other ***west*** to the Mediterranean. See Zechariah 14 verse 8. But there is more: "All the land shall be turned as a plain (JND, 'shall be turned as the Arabah'), from Geba to Rimmon south of Jerusalem: and it (Jerusalem) shall be lifted up, and inhabited in her place" (Zech. 14:10). The reference to the Arabah is deeply significant. It refers to the deep rift running from the sea of Galilee and the Jordan Valley, through the Dead Sea, to the Gulf of Aquaba. "Geba to Rimmon" is at present hill country, but it will be depressed to leave Jerusalem on an elevation in the centre of a plateau. The city will stand supreme before all, no matter from which direction they come.

The assembly should be similarly recognised. It should be a place where no obstacles are permitted to obscure its light. In fact, as "a city ... set on a hill" whose light "cannot be hid" (Matt. 5:14).

c) Its international position, v.1

"And people shall flow unto it" or 'And the peoples (plural) shall flow unto it" (JND). In the parallel passage, Isaiah writes, "And ***all nations*** shall flow unto it" (Isaiah 2:2). Prior to this, God will gather "all nations ***against*** Jerusalem to battle" (Zech. 14:2). W.E. Vine comments on the Isaiah passage as follows: 'A metaphor from the peaceful flowing of a river, in contrast to the tossings of the sea of national strife and upheaval'. Compare Isaiah 1 verse 8, "And the daughter of Zion is left as a cottage in a vineyard, as a lodge in a garden of cucumbers, as a beseiged city". There she is isolated and beseiged by enemies. But here, she is the centre of attraction and surrounded, not by enemies, but by admiring pilgrims from all over the world! These pilgrims from afar will not come with formal worship akin to Isaiah 1 verses 10-15, but like the Queen of Sheba. They will come as seekers after truth, desiring to be taught. Compare Isaiah 60 verse 3, "And the Gentiles shall come to thy light, and kings to the brightness of thy rising".

The assembly should be similarly recognised. It should be a place of attraction. It will not be attractive to the worldly or to the carnal, and is likely to arouse opposition from the religious world, but it should be attractive to the spiritual mind.

d) Its educational position, v.2

"And many nations shall come, and say, Come, and let us go up to the mountain of the LORD, and to the house of the ***God of Jacob***; and he will teach us of His ways, and we will walk in His paths: for the law shall go forth of Zion, and the word of the LORD from Jerusalem." It will be the university city of the world. There will be an evident desire to learn ("let us go up"), and a will to obey. This is education with a difference! Not the acquisition of information alone, but adjustment of life. Hence, "He will ***teach*** us of his ways, and we will ***walk*** in his paths". (The expressions "he will teach", v.2, and "neither shall they learn", v.3, express the positive and negative sides of the educational process.)

The words, "And many nations shall say" - not '***all*** nations shall say' - could indicate that there will be exceptions. If so, this is explained by Zechariah 14 verses 16-19: "And it shall be, that whoso will not come up of all the families of the earth unto Jerusalem to worship the King, the LORD of hosts, even upon them shall be no rain. And if the family of Egypt go not up, and come not, that have no rain, there shall be the plague". Even then, there will be some who 'forsake the assembling of themselves together!' (Heb. 10:25).

Jerusalem will also be the centre of universal worship. See Zechariah 14 verse 16, "And it shall come to pass, that every one that is left of all the nations which came against Jerusalem shall even go up from year to year to worship the King, the LORD of hosts, and to keep the feast of tabernacles". It will be characterised by divine holiness: "In that day shall there be upon the bells of the horses, HOLINESS UNTO THE LORD; and the pots of the LORD's house shall be like the bowls of the altar. Yea, every pot in Jerusalem and in Judah shall be holiness unto the LORD of hosts" (Zech. 14:20-21). Before this day dawns, Jerusalem will be called, "the great city, which spiritually is called Sodom and Egypt, where also our Lord was crucified" (Rev. 11:8).

The assembly should be similarly recognised. It should be a place of instruction where men speak "to edification (they ***build up***), and exhortation (they ***stir up***), and comfort (they ***cheer up***)" (1 Cor. 14:3). It should be a place where the overseer holds "fast the faithful word, as he hath been taught, that he may be able by sound doctrine both to exhort and to convince the gainsayers" (Titus 1:9). But it should also be a place where truth is obeyed, and saints "walk in his paths".

e) Its governmental position, v.3

"And he shall judge among many people, and rebuke strong nations afar off; and they shall beat their swords into plowshares, and their spears into pruninghooks: nation shall not lift up a sword against nation, neither shall they learn war any more." (Compare events before the battle of Armageddon as described in Joel 3:10, "Beat your plowshares into swords, and your pruninghooks into spears".) The United Nations will be redundant then, and there will be no question of calling on unwilling nations to respect Resolution XXX. Psalm 2 verse 9 makes it clear that no resistance will be permitted: "Thou shalt break them with a rod of iron; Thou shalt dash them in pieces like a potter's vessel".

It will be universal government that will ensure universal peace: "they shall beat their swords into plowshares, and their spears into pruninghooks". The entire world will be given to agricultural pursuits, and men will labour as God intended: "to dress it (the garden of Eden) and to keep it" (Gen. 2:15). The prophets speak eloquently on the subject. "And the desolate land shall be tilled, whereas it lay desolate in the sight of all that passed by. And they shall say, This land that was desolate is become like the garden of Eden; and the waste and desolate and ruined cities are become fenced and are inhabited" (Ezek 36:34-35). The same chapter stresses the fruitfulness of the mountains: "But ye, O mountains of Israel, ye shall shoot forth your branches, and yield your fruit to my people of Israel; for they are at hand to come. For, behold, I am for you, and I will turn unto you, and ye shall be tilled, and sown ... I will settle you after your old estates, and will do better unto you than at your beginnings" (Ezek.36:8-11). The agricultural achievements of Israel since its inauguration in 1948 are nothing less than amazing. But whilst we must be careful to give credit where it is indisputably due in this respect, it remains that the productivity of the land in the millennium will be a divine miracle. God will be actively for His people in every way. See Isaiah 35 verses 1-2, "The wilderness and the solitary place shall be glad for them (that is, "the ransomed of the Lord", v.10); and the desert shall rejoice, and blossom as the rose. It shall blossom abundantly, and rejoice even with joy and singing; the glory of Lebanon shall be given unto it, the excellency of Carmel and Sharon; they shall see the glory of the LORD, and the excellency of our God". The fertility of the land is described in Amos 9 verses 13-14, "Behold the days come, saith the LORD, that the ploughman shall overtake the reaper, and the treader of grapes him that soweth seed; and the mountains shall drop sweet wine, and all the hills shall melt". See also Jeremiah 31: "Thou shalt yet plant vines upon the mountains of Samaria: the planters shall plant, and shall eat them as common things ... They shall come and sing in the height of Zion, and shall flow together to the goodness of the LORD, for wheat, for wine, and for oil, and for the young of the flock and of the herd; and their soul shall be as a watered garden" (vv.5, 12).

Romans 8 makes clear that the tremendous changes in the world at this time await "the manifestation of the sons of God" (v.19). Until then, "the whole creation groaneth and travaileth in pain" (v.22). With the public display of the "sons of God", at the appearing on earth of the Lord Jesus Christ, creation itself "shall be delivered from the bondage of corruption into the glorious liberty of the children of God" (v.21). Colossians 1 verse 20 describes this as 'the reconciliation of all things to himself', and gives its basis: "the blood of his cross".

The assembly should be similarly recognised. It should be a place subject to godly government, where strife does not rear its head, and where spiritually agricultural pursuits are followed. After all, Paul described the assembly at Corinth as "God's husbandry" meaning 'tillage', 'cultivated field' or 'garden' (1 Cor. 3:9). Hence the figures of planting and watering.

Having seen something of the supremacy of the kingdom (vv.1-3), we should now notice:

2) THE SECURITY OF THE KINGDOM, vv.4-5

"But they shall sit every man under his vine and under his fig tree; and none shall make them afraid: for the mouth of the LORD of hosts hath spoken it." The strength of that security lies in the fact that "the LORD of hosts hath spoken it". In the days of Solomon, "Judah and Israel dwelt safely, every man under his vine and under his fig tree from Dan even to Beer-sheba" (1 Kings 4:25). But in the millennium it will be said, "Behold, a greater than Solomon is here!" (Matt. 12:42).

It has been suggested that verse 5 could be rendered, 'all the peoples do ***now*** walk in the name of their god, but we ***shall*** walk in the name of the LORD our God (Jehovah our Elohim) for ever'. The usual rendering implies that the godly remnant in Israel will enjoy God's rich millennial blessings because of their faithfulness. See Leviticus 26 verse 3, "If ye walk in my statutes, and keep my commandments, and do them, then I will give you rain in due season ... and I will give peace in the land, and ye shall lie down, and none shall make you afraid". So it is ***security through obedience.*** This brings us to:

3) THE STRENGTH OF THE KINGDOM, vv.6-8

"In that day, saith the LORD, will I assemble her that halteth, and I will gather her that is driven out, and her that I have afflicted; and I will make her that halted a remnant, and her that was cast far off a ***strong*** nation; and the Lord shall reign over them in mount Zion from henceforth, even for ever" (vv.6-7).

The word "halteth" means to limp, as in Genesis 32 verse 31: "he ***halted*** upon his thigh (Jacob's thigh)", as the "sun rose upon him". This is a significant picture! The scattered limping nation, under divine judgment - and more so when they accept Antichrist - will be regathered: "And I will make her that halteth a remnant". See Zephaniah 3 verses 12-13, "I will also leave in the midst of thee an afflicted and poor people, and they shall trust in the name of the LORD. The remant of Israel shall not do iniquity, nor speak lies; neither shall a deceitful tongue be found in their mouth: for they shall feed and lie down, and none shall make them afraid".

The prophets speak extensively of the regathering of the nation. See Jeremiah 31 verses 8-11, "Behold, I will bring them from the north country, and gather them from the coasts of the earth, and with them the blind and the lame, the woman with child and her that travaileth with child together: a great company shall return thither ... Hear the word of the LORD, O ye nations, and declare it in the isles afar off, and say, He that scattered Israel will gather him, and keep him, as a shepherd doth his flock. For the LORD hath redeemed Jacob, and ransomed him from the hand of him that was stronger than he".

The nation had often been warned through Moses that one consequence of disobedience would be scattering amongst the nations, and dispossession of their land. See Leviticus 26 verse 33, Deuteronomy 4 verses 26-27 and verses 63-68. The last passage has been fulfilled in our own lifetime, let alone in the coming tribulation: "And among these nations shalt thou find no ease, neither shall the soul of thy foot have rest ... and thy life shall hang in doubt before thee; and thou shalt fear day and night, and shalt have none assurance of thy life".

It is of course true that we see today a regathering in the land of God's earthly and acknowledged people. Undoubtedly this is necessary for the coming conflict in Israel: the stage is being set for future events. But this is not the regathering of Old Testament prophecy. The current success of

Israel must be attributed largely to the inherent genius of the nation: the future regathering will be solely by divine power. Note the following: "And it shall come to pass in that day, that the LORD shall set his hand again the second time to recover the remnant of his people ... and he shall set up an ensign for the nations, and shall assemble the outcasts of Israel, and gather together the dispersed of Judah from the four corners of the earth" (Isaiah 11:11-12). Compare Matthew 24 verse 31, "And he shall send his angels with a great sound of a trumpet (see Isaiah 27 verse 13 "And it shall come to pass in that day, that the great trumpet shall be blown, and they shall come which were ready to perish"), and they shall gather together his elect from the four winds, from one end of heaven to the other". See also Isaiah 43 verses 5-6, "Fear not, for I am with thee: I will bring thy seed from the east, and gather thee from the west; I will say to the north, Give up; and to the south, Keep not back: Bring my sons from far, and my daughters from the ends of the earth".

Israel will then be "the head, and not the tail" of the nations (Deut. 28:13). It will be "a strong nation" because "the Lord shall reign over them in mount Zion from henceforth, even for ever" (v.7). See Luke 1 verses 31-32, "He shall be great, and shall be called the Son of the Highest: and the Lord God shall give unto him the throne of his father David: and he shall reign over the house of Jacob for ever; and of his kingdom there shall be no end". Compare Isaiah 66 verse 22, "For as the new heavens and the new earth, which I will make, shall remain before me, saith the LORD, so shall your seed and your name remain".

The concluding verse of the paragraph emphasises the role of Jerusalem in the millennial reign of the Lord Jesus: "And thou, O tower of the flock, the strong hold of the daughter of Zion, unto thee shall it come, ***even the first dominion***; the kingdom shall come to the daughter of Jerusalem" (v.8). Towers of this nature were constructed to serve as shelters and watch towers for those employed to protect flocks. The expression, "tower of the flock", therefore conveys the idea of national security: God will watch over His flock.

MICAH

6) "He shall stand and feed in the strength of the LORD"

Read Chapter 4:9 - 5:15

As noted in our introduction, Chapters 1 & 2 can be entitled ***'Dispersion and Deliverance'*** ("For they are gone into captivity", Chapter 1:16; "The breaker is come up before them", Chapter 2:13), and Chapters 3:1 - 4:8 can be entitled ***'Ruin and Restoration'*** ("Therefore shall Zion for your sake be plowed as a field", Chapter 3:12; "The kingdom shall come to the daughter of Jerusalem", Chapter 4:8). These alternating paragraphs (sin and its consequences, followed by future blessing) continue in the third major section of the book (Chapters 4:9 - 5:15), which can be entitled ***'Travail and Triumph'***, in which the same alternation is repeated twice. The section divides into two sections of similar structure, each beginning and ending in the same way:

a) Chapter 4 verses 9-13 which begins with Israel's ***travail*** at the hands of her enemies (vv.9-10) ends with Israel's ***triumph*** over her enemies (vv.11-13). This section reveals the ***extent*** of Israel's travail.

b) Chapter 5 verses 1-15 which begins with Israel's ***travail*** at the hands of her enemies (v.1), continues with Israel's ***triumph*** over her enemies. This section gives the ***explanation*** of Israel's triumph.

1) THE EXTENT OF ISRAEL'S TRAVAIL, 4:9-13

Israel's "travail" (v.9) commences with the Babylonian captivity (v.10), and ends with a colossal invasion at the end-time: "Now also many nations are gathered against thee" (v.11).

i) It begins with captivity to Babylon, 4:9-10. The previous section concluded with the words, "The kingdom shall come to the daughter of Jerusalem" (4:8), but there is no kingdom in verse 9, only captivity. "Be in pain, and labour to bring forth, O daughter of Zion, like a woman in ***travail*** ... thou shalt go even to Babylon". This marks the commencement of the "times of the Gentiles", when God placed the government of the world in Gentile hands. While the latter part of verse 10 ("There shalt thou be delivered; there the LORD shall redeem thee from the hand of thine enemies") may well anticipate, in part, the return from Babylon in the days of Zerubbabel and Ezra, its complete fulfilment must be future. This is clear from the fact that verses 11-13 have not yet been fulfilled: the daughter of Zion has not yet arisen and threshed (v.13). But her travail will end, and she will be victorious over every enemy.

ii) It ends with victory over many nations, 4:11-13. The deliverance described in verses 9-10 which anticipates the period of travail, also anticipates its ***end***: "***There*** the LORD shall redeem thee from the hand of thine enemies". As already noted, in its fullest extent the passage does not refer to the return after seventy years in exile as described in the books of Ezra and Nehemiah, but to deliverance from Gentile domination headed by Babylon.

We learn more about the final form of Israel's travail, and her deliverance in verses 11-13: "Now also many nations are gathered against thee, that say, Let her be defiled, and let our eye look upon Zion". We should notice that like the Assyrian in Isaiah 10 verses 5-6, the nations will unconsciously implement the will of God: "they know not the thoughts of the LORD, neither understand they his counsel: for ***he*** shall gather them as the sheaves into the floor" (v.12). Compare Zechariah 14 verse 2 ("***I*** will gather all nations to Jerusalem to battle"), and Revelation 16 verses 13-16 ("And I saw three unclean spirits like frogs come out of the mouth of the dragon ... the beast ... the false prophet. For they are the spirits of devils, working miracles, which go forth unto the kings of the earth and of the whole world, to gather them to the battle of that great day of God Almighty ... And ***he*** gathered them together into a place called in the Hebrew tongue Armageddon"). Notice that in both these passages, it is God Himself who gathers the nations. At the time of "Jacob's trouble" (Jer. 30:7), when all seems lost, Israel's Messiah will return (Zech. 14:3-4), and Israel will "arise and thresh" (v.13). Their victory will be accomplished by divine power: "***I*** will make thine horn iron, and ***I*** will make thy hoofs brass: and thou shalt beat in pieces many people" (v.13). Compare Zechariah 12 verse 3: "And in that day will ***I*** make Jerusalem a burdensome stone for all people: all that burden themselves with it shall be cut to pieces, though all people of the earth be gathered together against it". The words, "And ***I*** will consecrate their gain unto the LORD, and their substance unto the Lord of the whole earth" (v.13) are amplified in Zechariah

14 verse 14: “and the wealth of the heathen round about shall be gathered together, gold, and silver, and apparel, in great abundance”. The speaker in verse 13 (“I”) is Israel’s Messiah.

In summary, Israel’s travail covers an extended period. It has already lasted some 2,500 years. It began with the Babylonian captivity, and will end with the unparalleled suffering of the Great Tribulation. See Jeremiah 30 verses 6-7 (“Ask ye now, and see whether a man doth travail with child? Wherefore do I see every man with his hands on his loins, as a woman in travail, and all faces turned into paleness? Alas, for that day is great, so that none is like it: it is even the time of Jacob’s trouble: but he shall be saved out of it”); Daniel 12 verse 1 (“There shall be a time of trouble such as never was since there was a nation even to that same time”); Matthew 24 verses 21-22 (“For there shall be great tribulation, such as was not since the beginning of the world to this time, no, nor ever shall be”).

2) THE EXPLANATION OF ISRAEL’S TRIUMPH, 5:1-15

Chapter 5 verse 1, which is actually part of chapter 4 in the Hebrew text (see JND margin note), re-introduces the capture of Jerusalem by the Babylonians described in Chapter 4 verse 10. It does so in order to contrast what would happen then with what would happen in the future. Keil & Delitzsch put it like this: “The divine exaltation of the future Ruler of Israel is contrasted with the deepest degradation of the judge”. We must therefore notice: ***(a)*** the humiliation of “the judge of Israel” (v.1) and ***(b)*** the glory of the “ruler in Israel” (vv.2-15).

a) The humiliation of “the judge of Israel”, v.1

“Now gather thyself in troops, O daughter of troops; he hath laid siege against us; they shall smite the judge of Israel with a rod upon the cheek.” Whilst other explanations have been suggested, it seems most likely that the “troops” refer to the mustering of the soldiers in the defence of the city. But to no avail for “they (the besieging enemy) shall smite the judge of Israel with a rod upon the cheek”. This certainly implies that the enemy had entered the city. The title “judge of Israel” evidently refers to the king since it refers to ‘the person holding the highest office in Israel’ (Keil & Deitzsch). See 1 Samuel 8 verses 5-6, “now make us a king to judge us like all the nations. But the thing displeased Samuel, when they said, Give us a king to judge us”. To “smite … with a rod upon the cheek” was the highest insult. See 1 Kings 22 verse 24. The Lord

Jesus was treated in this way: “Then they did spit in his face, and buffeted him; and other smote him with the palms of their hands … And they spit upon him, and took the reed and smote him on the head” (Matt. 26:67; 27:30).

The last king of Judah was Zedekiah of whom it was said, “And thou, profane wicked prince, whose day is come, when iniquity shall have an end … Remove the diadem, and take off the crown; … I will overturn, overturn, overturn it; and it shall be no more, until he come whose right it is; and I will give it him” (Ezek. 21:25-27). Zedekiah was utterly humiliated; the last thing he saw was the execution of his sons, after which his eyes were put out and he was taken to Babylon in chains (2 Kings 25:6-7).

But this was not the end for Israel or for the throne of David. The chapter continues by describing the advent of a glorious “ruler in Israel” (v.2).

b) The glory of the “ruler in Israel”, vv.2-15

The passage describes ***(i)*** His first coming (v.2); ***(ii)*** the interval between His comings (v.3); ***(iii)*** His second coming (vv.4-15). Between the two advents lies a period in which the Lord would not be present amongst His people (“therefore shall he give them up”, meaning ‘leave them to suffer their calamities’, *Pulpit Commentary*) which would terminate with Israel’s future travail (v.3).

i) His first coming, v.2

We should notice:

- His humanity. “But thou, Bethlehem Ephratah, though thou be little among the thousands of Judah, yet ***out of thee*** shall he come forth unto me ...” The words, “little among the thousands of Judah”, indicate the humble circumstances of His birth. Bearing in mind that Bethlehem was the birthplace of David, the shepherd-king (Psalm 78:70-72), it is fitting that this prediction should be given through Micah, whose prophecy emphasises Messiah’s shepherd character. It is not without significance that when He came, there were “shepherds ... keeping watch over their flock”. The New Testament reminds us that He “was made of the seed of David according to the flesh” (Rom. 1:3). The “living bread which came down from heaven” (John 6:51) was born in Bethlehem, ‘the house of bread.’ The “corn of wheat” who brought forth “much fruit” (John 12:24) was found in Ephratah, meaning ‘fruitful’ or ‘fertility’. We should add that the name Bethlehem Ephratah distinguishes the town from other places bearing the name Bethlehem (see Joshua 19:15, referring to a village in Zebulun), so emphasising the pin-point accuracy of Scripture.

- ***His piety.*** "Come forth ***unto me***." This emphasises the character of His life. He was at all times well-pleasing to God. Compare Isaiah 53 verse 2 ("grow up ***before him***"). It has been said that the Father proclaimed His pleasure in His Son in connection with His ***preparation*** (Matt. 3:17), His ***presentation*** (Matt. 17:5) and His ***passion*** (John 12:28).

- ***His deity.*** "Whose goings forth have been from of old, ***from everlasting***." (Note: the priests and scribes omitted these words when answering Herod (Matt. 2:5-6): it would not have been diplomatic to mention that the expected King would be divine.) Compare Isaiah 9 verse 6: the "child" was born at Bethlehem, but the "Son" was "from everlasting". He is "the mighty God, the everlasting Father". The margin reading "from the days of eternity" (supported by JND) should be compared with "the days of his flesh" (Heb. 5:7). "The Word was made flesh, and dwelt among us" (John 1:14). ***See Addenda (1).***

ii) The interval between His comings, v.3

"Therefore will he give them up, until the time that she which travaileth hath brought forth." The word "therefore" has been subject to some long explanations, but it does seem to refer to the circumstances which gave rise to the captivity. Israel would be 'given up' or left to suffer, until "the time that she which travaileth ***hath brought forth***". Alternatively the word "therefore" could simply mean, 'because of His settled plan' (Jamieson, Fausset & Brown). Israel will pass through the untold pain and agony of "Jacob's trouble" (Jer. 30:7), out of which will come a new nation. Compare Isaiah 66 verse 8, "Who hath heard such a thing? who hath seen such things? Shall the earth be made to bring forth in one day? Or shall a nation be born at once? for as soon as Zion ***travailed***, she ***brought forth*** her children". ***See Addenda (2)***. This will be followed by the return to the land by Jews from all over the world: "then the remnant of his brethren shall return unto the children of Israel". This is described in Matthew 24 verses 30-31.

iii) His second coming, vv.4-15

At His second coming He will preserve His people (vv.4-6), promote His people (vv.7-9) and purify His people (vv.10-15).

a) The preservation of His people, vv.4-6

He shall "stand and feed", v.4. Notice His shepherd character (compare 2:12; 4:8; 7:14) together with the dignity of His ministry. It will be "in the strength of the LORD, in the majesty of the name of the LORD his God". It is not surprising to notice the result of such ministry: ***"they shall abide!"*** Let every elder take note. Caring for the flock of God should never be undertaken light-heartedly. He will fulfil Ezekiel 34 verses 11, 22-23, "For thus saith the Lord GOD; Behold, I, even I, will both search my sheep, and seek them out ... Therefore will I save my flock, and they shall no more be a prey ... And I will set up one shepherd over them, and he shall feed them".

He shall "be great", v.4. Compare Luke 1 verses 32-33. He is greater than Jonah, greater than Solomon (Matthew 12:41-42), and greater than the temple (Matthew 12:6). He is a "great prophet": He is "the great king". He is "a great high priest". He is "the great God". He is "that great shepherd of the sheep". Whilst we gladly acknowledge this ***now***, the whole world will acknowledge His greatness when He has "dominion from sea to sea, and from the river unto the ends of the earth" (Psalm 72:8).

He shall "be the peace", vv.5-6. Literally, "And this [man] shall be Peace" (JND). The prophetic scriptures abound with descriptions of world peace when "the Prince of Peace" reigns. See, for example, Isaiah 2 verse 4; 32 verse 17; 66 verse 12. Note Jeremiah 23 verse 6, "In his days Judah shall be saved, and Israel shall dwell safely". Micah describes here the peace of God's people when invaded at the end-time by the last Assyrian. He will evidently come from the region occupied by the past Assyrian, and Ezekiel 38-39 could possibly refer to this invasion. Note the connection between Nimrod and Assyria in Genesis 10 verses 8-11. While the word "waste" (v.6) is sometimes translated 'shepherd', here it has the meaning of 'consume' or 'eat up' (AV margin).

He shall "deliver us", v.6. The "seven shepherds and eight principal (princely) men" (v.5) should be compared to the past shepherds described in Jeremiah 23 verses 1-6: "Woe be to the pastors that destroy and scatter the sheep of my pasture! saith the LORD ... And I will set up shepherds over them which shall feed them: and they shall fear no more, nor be dismayed, neither shall they be lacking, saith the LORD". The words "***seven*** shepherds" could refer to the completeness of shepherd care, and "***eight*** principal men" could refer to a totally new character of rule, bearing in mind that eight indicates the commencement of something new. *The Pulpit Commentary* explains this as follows: "The instrumentality that He employs may seem to us very feeble. 'Seven shepherds and eight principal men' against unnumbered hosts of the enemies. 'He chooseth the foolish things of the world to confound the wise' etc (1 Cor. 1:27). Though the instrumentality may seem feeble, it was sufficient. The work was done 'Not by might, nor by power, but by my Spirit, saith the Lord' (Zech 4:6)".

b) The promotion of His people, vv.7-9

The nations of the world will rise or fall by their relationship with the Jew. Here we have the ultimate fulfilment of the promise in Genesis 12 verses 1-3, where God said: ***"I will bless them that bless thee"***. This will be completely fulfilled in the future: "And the remnant of Jacob shall be in the midst of many people ***as a dew from the LORD***, as the showers upon the grass, that tarrieth not for man, nor waiteth for the sons of men" (v.7). (Dew and rain cannot be delayed, and God's blessing will not be delayed either.) Compare Zechariah 8 verse 13, "And it shall come to pass, that as ye were a curse among the heathen, O house of Judah, and house of Israel; so will I save you, and ye ***shall be a blessing***". In addition, Gentiles will evidently be employed in evangelising the world: Isaiah 66 verses 19-20 tells us that the Gentiles that survive the catastrophic defeat at Jerusalem will be "sent unto the nations, to Tarshish, Pul, and Lud, that draw the bow, to Tubal and Javan, to the isles afar off, that have not heard my fame, neither have seen my glory; and they shall declare my glory among the Gentiles. And they shall bring all your brethren for an offering unto the Lord out of all nations".

"I will ... curse him that curseth thee." This too will be fulfilled in the future: "And the remnant of Jacob shall be among the Gentiles in the midst of many people as a lion among the beasts of the forest, ***as a young lion among the flocks of sheep***: who, if he go through, both treadeth down, and teareth in pieces, and none can deliver. Thine hand shall be lifted up upon thine adversaries, and all thine enemies shall be cut off" (vv.8-9).

c) The purification of His people, vv.10-15

"And it shall come to pass in that day, saith the LORD, that I will cut off thy horses out of the midst of thee." Compare Isaiah 4 where God describes the holiness of His people after He has "purged the blood of Jerusalem from the midst thereof by the spirit of judgment, and by the spirit of burning" (v.4). "Micah writes of a day when the nation would be purified of its sin and maintained in an attitude of pure and intense devotion to God. She would give up trust in foreign military alliances (vv.10-11), the occult (v.12) and false gods (vv.13-14)" (James Montgomery Boice, *The Minor Prophets*). In short, Israel will be purged of everything in which she had trusted for security. Compare Zechariah 13 verse 2, "And it shall come to pass in that day, saith the LORD of hosts, that I will cut off the names of the idols out of the land, and they shall no more be remembered: and also I will cause the prophets and the unclean spirit to pass out of the land".

The final verse (v.15) reminds us of 1 Peter 4 verse 17, "For the time is come that judgment must begin at the house of God: and if it first begin at us, what shall the end be of them that obey not the gospel of God?"

Addenda

(1)

(Taken from Richard Catchpole's December 2003 Newsletter)

"But thou, Bethlehem Ephratah, though thou be little among the thousands of Judah, yet out of thee shall he come forth unto me that is to be ruler in Israel; whose goings forth have been from of old, from everlasting" (Micah 5:2).

Although only seven chapters, the prophecy of Micah is particularly rich in its presentation of the glories of Christ, and its promises regarding the restoration of the nation of Israel. In Chapter 4 the focus is upon the character of the deliverance, and Millennial conditions are described, but in Chapter 5 the key theme is the coming of the Deliverer. We have in this well-known verse a notable prophecy concerning the birth of Christ, specifically identifying the place where Messiah would be born. But it is not so much the place that occupies our attention as the Person who would come out from there.

The verse indicates that we are thinking of a Man: "out of thee shall he come forth". Since verse 3 speaks about the "remnant of his brethren", this reminds us of ***Luke's*** presentation of Christ as the Son of Man, the perfect Man.

But the verse continues: “out of thee shall he come forth unto me”. This is One who would come forth, to do and accomplish the will and purpose of God - “unto me” - which reminds us surely of ***Mark’s*** presentation of Christ as the perfect Servant.

Again, this One “is to be ruler in Israel”, which forges an immediate link with the Gospel of ***Matthew*** and the presentation of Christ as the Son of David, the Sovereign, born king of the Jews.

Finally we are told, “whose goings forth *have been* from of old, from everlasting”. That is of course ***John’s*** Gospel, where Christ is seen to be the eternal Son of God. He was coming forth from Bethlehem Ephratah, but that was not His beginning, His goings forth were from eternity.

There is a time coming when in the language of verse 4, He shall “be great unto the ends of the earth”, and as we come to the close of another year we can thank God that His decree concerning Christ will yet be fulfilled.

(2)

Isaiah 66 also refers to a birth ***before*** the ultimate travail of Israel. Before saying, “as soon as Zion travaileth she brought forth her children” (v.8), (indicating the shortness of the tribulation: “except those days were shortened”), we read, “***Before*** she travaileth she brought forth; before her pain came she was delivered of a ***man child”*** (v.7). It is ***singular***: man child, as opposed to the ***plural***: children, or sons. This is explained in Revelation 12, where Israel is described, not in all her moral and spiritual corruption, but as the centre of divine administration and glory: “A woman clothed with the sun, and the moon under her feet, and upon her head, a crown of twelve stars” (v.1). Israel’s future glory derives from the reign of her greatest Son: “She brought forth a man child, who was to rule all nations with a rod of iron” (v.5). There is no doubting His identity. See Psalm 2 verses 7-9: “The LORD hath said unto me, Thou art my Son; this day have I begotten thee … thou shalt break them with a rod of iron”. It is not therefore surprising to read that Satan attempts to destroy the Child born, and so frustrate God’s plans. The reference, “as soon it was born”, clearly points to Matthew 2, and the murder of all children under age of two. The reason for the complete omission of any other detail concerning the “man child, who was to rule all nations with a rod of iron”, is explained by the chapter. God has not in view here the life, death and resurrection of His beloved Son, but ***His future rule***, and Satan’s attempt to frustrate it.

MICAH

7) "He hath shewed thee, O man, what is good"

Read Chapter 6:1-16

Chapter 6 verse 1 – Chapter 7 verse 20 represents the fourth major division of the book and can be entitled ***'Forgetfulness and Faithfulness'***. For 'forgetfulness', see Chapter 6 verse 5: "O my people, remember …"; for 'faithfulness', see Chapter 7 verse 20: "Thou wilt perform the truth to Jacob …" Chapter 6 describes God's ***controversy*** with His people: "The LORD hath a controversy with his people" (v.2). Chapter 7 describes God's ***compassion*** on His people: "He will have compassion upon us" (v.19).

Chapter 6 may be analysed as follows: ***(1)*** God's controversy with His people (vv.1-3); ***(2)*** God's care for His people (vv.4-5); ***(3)*** God's requirement of His people (vv.6-8); ***(4)*** God's chastening of His people (vv.9-16).

1) GOD'S CONTROVERSY WITH HIS PEOPLE, vv.1-3

The section begins with reference to the "mountains" and "hills": "Hear ye now what the LORD saith; Arise, contend (meaning, 'plead your case in court') thou before the mountains, and let the hills hear thy voice. Hear ye, O mountains, the LORD'S controversy, and ye strong foundations of the earth: for the LORD hath a controversy with his people, and he will plead with Israel" (vv.1-2). The Lord calls on permanent and immoveable witnesses to observe His controversy with Israel. The "mountains" and "hills" would listen to them (v.1) and to Him (v.2.). The Lord then makes His case: "O my people, what have I done unto thee? and wherein have I ***wearied*** thee? testify against me" (v.3). Their behaviour suggested that He had failed them. There is deep pathos in the words, "O ***my people***". Three centuries later, His people blatantly despised divine ordinances, saying, "The table of the LORD is polluted; and the fruit thereof, even his meat, is contemptible. Ye said also, Behold, what a ***weariness*** is it!" (Mal. 1:12-13). Do ***we*** say in effect, by attitude and conduct, "What a weariness is it"? Their conduct implied that the Lord was deficient and could not be trusted or satisfy His people. Compare Jeremiah 2 verse 5: "What iniquity have your fathers found in me, that they are gone far from me, and have walked after vanity, and are become vain?" We tend to forget that backsliding is offensive to ***God.*** It is a reproach to Him. It is distrust of His love and care.

But although God says, "Testify against me", no grounds existed for any possible charge against Him, and He now validates His claim to call them "my people". He will never forget His covenant with them (7:18-20), but they had forgotten:

2) GOD'S CARE FOR HIS PEOPLE, vv.4-5

This is expressed in three ways ***(a)*** divine power at the beginning of the journey from Egypt to Canaan (v.4); ***(b)*** divine provision during the journey (v.4); ***(c)*** divine protection at the end of the journey (v.5).

a) Divine power, v.4

Note the reference to events at the ***beginning*** of the journey from Egypt to Canaan: "I brought thee up out of the land of Egypt, and redeemed thee out of the house of servants (i.e. slavery)". They experienced redemption and deliverance from bondage. The Lord Jesus described a worse kind of bondage in John 8 verse 34: "Whosoever committeth sin is the servant (*doulos*, slave) of sin". Sadly, Israel failed to recognise that redemption carried obligations. See Judges 6 verses 8 and 10, "Thus saith the LORD God of Israel, I brought you up from Egypt, and brought you forth out of the house of bondage ... but ye have ***not*** obeyed my voice", and Isaiah 43 verse 1, "I have redeemed thee, I have called thee by thy name; thou art mine". The New Testament is equally emphatic: "Pass the time of your sojourning here in fear: forasmuch as ye know that ye were not redeemed with corruptible things, as silver and gold … but with the precious blood of Christ" (1 Pet. 1:17-19). Note the implications in 1 Corinthians 6 verse 20, "For ye are bought with a price: therefore ***glorify God*** in your body". The Passover was an annual reminder of redemption. The Lord's supper should be a constant reminder of ***our*** redemption, and the obligations which rest upon redeemed people. Notice the connection between the passover and the feast of unleavened bread in 1 Corinthians 5 verses 7-8.

b) Divine provision, v.4

Notice now the reference to events ***during*** the journey from Egypt to Canaan: "I sent before thee Moses, Aaron, and Miriam". Moses was a ***prophet.*** He had the word of God. See Deuteronomy 34 verse 10, "And there arose not a prophet since in Israel like unto Moses, whom the LORD knew face to face". This reminds us that we are to "remember them which have the rule over you, who have spoken unto you the word of God; whose faith follow" (Heb. 13:7). Aaron was the ***priest.*** Israel enjoyed the priestly facility expressed in Hebrews 5 verse 1, "For every high priest taken from among men is ordained ***for*** men in things pertaining ***to*** God". Miriam is connected with ***praise.*** See Exodus 15 verses 20-21. She is described as "the prophetess" and evidently led the praise of the women who "went out after her with timbrels and with dances". It should be noted that she repeated the words of Moses: compare Exodus 15 verse 1. She is described as "the sister of Aaron", not 'the sister of Moses'. Priesthood and praise certainly go hand in hand! Perhaps the words, "I sent before thee Moses, Aaron, and Miriam", indicate that there was leadership for all, both men and women. The Lord Jesus fills all three offices: He is the "great prophet" (Luke 7:16); He is our "great high priest" (Heb. 4:14); He is the leader of the praise: "in the midst of the church will I sing praise unto thee" (Heb. 2:12).

c) Divine protection, v.5

Note the reference to events at the ***end*** of the journey from Egypt to Canaan. "O my people, remember now what Balak king of Moab consulted, and what Balaam the son of Beor answered him from ***Shittim*** (the last place of encampment before the passage of Jordan) unto ***Gilgal*** (the first place of encampment after the passage of Jordan)." Balak required Balaam to curse Israel: "Behold, I have received commandment to bless; and he hath blessed; and I cannot reverse it. He hath not beheld iniquity in Jacob, neither hath he seen perverseness in Israel" (Num. 23:20-21). Balaam was obliged to say: "How goodly are thy tents, O Jacob, and thy tabernacles, O Israel" (Num. 24:5). Such is God's estimate of His people!

All this substantiates the statement, "that ye may know the righteousness of the LORD". That is, He cannot be prevailed upon to alter His attitude to His people, ***although*** His people can be prevailed upon to alter their attitude to Him. See Numbers 25 verses 1-18 and Chapter 31 verses 1-20. God's purposes are immutable. See Romans 8 verses 29-30, "For whom he did foreknow, he also did predestinate to be conformed to the image of his Son, that he might be the firstborn among many brethren. Moreover whom he did predestinate, them he also called: and whom he called, them he also justified: and whom he justified, them he also glorified".

In view of God's righteous dealings with them, how should they have behaved? This brings us to:

3) GOD'S REQUIREMENT OF HIS PEOPLE, vv.6-8

If Israel had ***forgotten*** her redemption and subsequent events (vv.4-5), it follows that she had also forgotten the standard of conduct appropriate to redeemed people, and the question is asked, "Wherewith shall I come before the LORD, and bow myself before the high God?" (v.6). God required reality. He required consistency of life, as opposed to external ritual and ceremony. We must now notice what the Lord did not require (vv.6-7) and what He did require (v.8).

a) What God did not require, vv.6-7

The Lord Jesus told the woman of Samaria that "they that worship him (the Father) must worship him in spirit and in truth" (John 4:24). They were offering ***(i)*** Levitical sacrifices (v.6-7a), but these were not "in spirit": they were orthodox, but completely lacking in real devotion to the Lord. They were offering ***(ii)*** pagan sacrifices (v.7b), but these were not "in truth": they were horribly idolatrous. Both are described as follows:

i) Their Levitical sacrifices were unacceptable. "Shall I come before him with burnt-offerings, with calves of a year old? Will the LORD be pleased with thousands of rams, or with ten thousands of rivers of oil?" However orthodox, they were unacceptable because they were devoid of ***reality***. External formality is worthless without the practical godliness described in verse 8. Compare Isaiah 1 verses 11-17. Read Psalm 51 verses 16-17: "Thou desirest not sacrifice, else would I give it: thou delightest not in burnt offering. The sacrifices of God are a broken spirit: a broken and a contrite heart, O God, thou wilt not despise". Samuel made this clear to Saul: "Hath the LORD as great delight in burnt offerings and sacrifices, as in obeying the voice of the LORD? Behold, to obey is better than sacrifice, and to hearken than the fat of rams" (1 Sam. 15:22).

ii) Their pagan sacrifices were unacceptable. "Shall I give my firstborn for my transgression, the fruit of my body for the sin of my soul?" This refers to practices in the reign of wicked Ahab. "He … made his son to pass through the fire (in honour of Molech), according to the abominations of the heathen" (2 Kings 16:3).

b) What God did require, v.8

"He hath shewed thee, O man, what is good; and what doth the LORD require of thee, but to do justly, and to love mercy, and to walk humbly with thy God?" We must look at this in two ways: ***(i)*** God's requirements of His people; ***(ii)*** God's requirements seen perfectly in Christ.

i) God's requirements of His people

- *"To do justly."* The word is used widely in the Old Testament. See, for example, Deuteronomy 16 verse 19, "Thou shalt not wrest ***judgment***: thou shalt not respect persons, neither take a gift: for a gift doth blind the eyes of the wise, and pervert the words of the righteous". See also Leviticus 19 verses 15 and 35. So there was to be complete equity, honesty and integrity. We may not be open to bribery and corruption, but it is not unknown for decisions affecting assembly life to be influenced by family and social considerations. The word is used in Proverbs 16 verse 11 with reference to business transactions: "A ***just*** weight and balance are the LORD'S". God's word must govern ***all*** our relationships, and ***every*** aspect of our lives.

- *"To love mercy."* This is a divine characteristic. The same word is used in Micah 7 verse 18, "He retaineth not his anger for ever, because he delighteth in ***mercy***". It was a lesson that Jonah sorely needed to learn! See Jonah 4. Scholars suggest that the word "mercy" conveys the idea of 'lovingkindness'. We are exhorted to be "kind one to another, tender-hearted, forgiving one another" (Eph. 4:32). It is most important to maintain "all the counsel of God", but we must do so in the right way. It is sadly possible to be completely orthodox, but so hard with it! There was little mercy in Micah's day, where the princes "eat the flesh of my people, and flay their skin from off them; and they break their bones, and chop them in pieces, as for the pot" (3:1-3). We must be careful not to practise spiritual cannibalism (Gal. 5:15).

- *"To walk humbly with thy God."* The New Testament abounds with teaching on this subject, which emphasises its necessity and importance. For example, “Let nothing be done through strife or vain glory; but in lowliness of mind let each esteem other better than themselves” (Phil. 2:3). Humility is essentially an attitude of mind. If pride exhibits itself in self-assertion, then humility exhibits itself in self-denial. We should notice the Lord’s teaching in this connection: “Except ye be converted, and become as little children, ye shall not enter into the kingdom of heaven. Whosoever therefore shall humble himself as this little child, the same is greatest (perhaps ‘greater’: see JND margin) in the kingdom of heaven” (Matt. 18:3-4).

ii) God’s requirements seen perfectly in Christ

He did “justly”, He loved “mercy” and He walked “humbly”.

- ***He did “justly”.*** There was no inequity in His dealings with rich and poor. He displayed no bias towards the higher strata of Jewish society. The crowds “murmured, saying, That he was gone to be guest with a man that is a sinner” (Luke 19:7). He faithfully condemned religious hypocrisy. He was equally faithful at Jacob’s well, saying to the woman, “Thou hast had five husbands; and he whom thou now hast is not thy husband” (John 4:17-18).

- ***He loved “mercy”.*** This is made abundantly clear in John 8 verse 11: “Neither do I condemn thee: go, and sin no more”. Blind Bartimaeus proved that the Lord Jesus loved mercy: His cry, “Jesus, thou Son of David, have mercy on me” (Mark 10:47), was wonderfully answered. The Lord Jesus completely fulfilled the ancient prophecy, “A bruised reed shall he not break, and the smoking flax shall he not quench” (Isaiah 42:3; Matt. 12:20).

- ***He walked “humbly”.*** The Lord Jesus never sought publicity, and He never performed a miracle for His own benefit. After the healing of the deaf and dumb man, “he charged them that they should tell no man” (Mark 7:36). After the transfiguration, “he charged them that they should tell no man what things they had seen, till the Son of man were risen from the dead” (Mark 9:9). He said, “the Lord GOD hath given me the tongue of the learned … he wakeneth morning by morning, he wakeneth mine ear to hear as the learned” (Isaiah 50:4). He always waited the Father’s time. Hence we read, “Wherefore ***God*** also hath highly exalted Him” (Phil. 2: 9).

The final paragraph in this chapter is introduced by the words, “The LORD’S voice crieth unto the city, and the man of wisdom shall see thy name: hear ye the rod, and who hath appointed it". It deals with:

4) GOD'S CHASTENING OF HIS PEOPLE, vv.9-16

The use of the rod is predicted: "Hear ye the rod, and who hath appointed it (v.9) ... Therefore also will I make thee sick in smiting thee" (v.13).

a) The recognition of chastening, v.9

A wise man recognises divine discipline, and its necessity. "The LORD'S voice crieth unto the city, and the man of wisdom shall see thy name." This is elsewhere translated, 'And wisdom looketh on thy name' (JND). Whilst this passage deals with divine judgment on sin, we must not forget that God disciplines His people in order to produce still greater conformity to His mind and will. Hebrews 12 verses 5-13 is compulsory reading on this subject.

b) The reason for chastening, vv.10-13

The conditions required by the Lord ("to do justly, and to love mercy, and to walk humbly with thy God", v.8) were lacking in God's people:

- ***They did not "do justly".*** "Are there yet the treasures of wickedness in the house of the wicked, and scant measure that is abominable? Shall I count them pure with the wicked balances, and with the bag of deceitful weights?" (vv.10-11). There were "treasures of wickedness" through "scant measure". In other words, ill-gotten gains through malpractices in business. There were "wicked balances" and "deceitful weights". Solomon rightly said that "a false balance is abomination to the LORD: but a just weight is his delight" (Prov. 11:1). See also Proverbs 16 verse 11, "A just weight and balance are the LORD'S: all the weights of the bag are his work".

- ***They did not "love mercy".*** It was quite the reverse: "For the rich men thereof are full of violence" (v.12).

- ***They did not "walk humbly".*** They were given to "lies, and their tongue is deceitful in their mouth" (v.12).

Divine judgment was inevitable: "***Therefore*** also will I make thee sick in smiting thee, in making thee desolate because of thy sins" (v.13).

c) The result of chastening, vv.14-16

God's people would be left with unfulfilled expectations. "Thou shalt eat, but ***not*** be satisfied; and thy casting down shall be in the midst of thee; and thou shalt take hold ('of loved ones and possessions', M.C. Unger), but shalt ***not*** deliver ('rescue them from the invading enemy', M.C. Unger); and that which thou deliverest will I give up to the sword. Thou shalt sow, but thou shalt ***not*** reap; thou shalt tread the olives, but thou shalt ***not*** anoint thyself with oil; and sweet wine, but shalt ***not*** drink wine" (vv.14-15). Disaster would overtake them when everything looked so promising. These verses recall Haggai 1 verses 6 and 9. We cannot expect the "joy of the Lord" to be our strength (Neh. 8:10), if we live without Him.

Sadly, Judah had not learnt from the history of Israel. "The statutes of Omri (he established Samaria as Israel's capital) are kept, and all the works of the house of Ahab, and ye walk in ***their*** counsels" (v.16). Although Israel was now in captivity, Judah remained influenced and contaminated by the infection she contracted through compromise. See, for example, 2 Chronicles 21 verse 6, Jehoram "walked in the way of the kings of Israel, like as did the house of Ahab: for he had the daughter of Ahab to wife". Compromise leads to disaster: "Ye walk in ***their*** counsels; that I should make thee a desolation, and the inhabitants thereof an hissing (derision: see Lam. 2:15): therefore ye shall bear the reproach of my people". The "reproach of my people" is best explained by such passages as Jeremiah 22 verses 8-9: "And many nations shall pass by this city, and they shall say every man to his neighbour, Wherefore hath the LORD done thus unto this great city? Then they shall answer, Because they have forsaken the covenant of the LORD their God, and worshipped other gods, and served them".

It would be a terrible tragedy if men and women said something similar about us.

MICAH

8) "Who is a God like unto thee?"

Read Chapter 7:1-20

We have already noticed that Chapter 6 verse 1 – Chapter 7 verse 20 represents the fourth major division of the book, and can be entitled ***'Forgetfulness and Faithfulness'***. Chapter 6 describes God's ***controversy*** with His people (v.2) and Chapter 7 describes God's ***compassion*** on His people (v.19). Micah 7 may be divided as follows: ***(1)*** Micah's current circumstances (vv.1-7); ***(2)*** Israel's coming captivity (vv.8-10); ***(3)*** Israel's certain regathering (vv.11-17); ***(4)*** God's covenant mercy (vv.18-20). The chapter follows the familiar pattern of ruin (vv.1-7), retribution (vv.8-10), and restoration (vv.11-20).

1) MICAH'S CURRENT CIRCUMSTANCES, vv.1-7

Chapter 6 ends with the chilling words, "The statutes of Omri are kept, and all the works of the house of Ahab, and ye walk in their counsels". The reign of Omri is described in 1 Kings 16 verses 23-29. He "did worse than all that were before him" (v.25). We learn from the commencement of Chapter 7 that the situation in Judah caused Micah considerable distress. It was impossible to trust anyone in society, however near and dear (vv.1-6), and the prophet had no alternative but to trust completely in God (v.7).

a) Men are faithless, vv.1-6

"Woe is me! for I am as when they have gathered the summer fruits, as the grapegleanings of the vintage: there is no cluster to eat: my soul desired the firstripe fruit" (v.1). While these words evidently introduce Micah's personal lament, they clearly reflect the deep feelings of God Himself. The prophet looked for good and upright men amongst his contemporaries and found none. It was comparable to a vineyard stripped completely bare, with nothing left for the gleaners (Deut. 24:21). Compare Jeremiah 5 verses 1-5. God's vineyard had "brought forth wild grapes" (Isa. 5:1-2). Every part of society was affected.

- He had no confidence in men generally. "The good man ('godly [man]', JND) is perished out of the earth: and there is none upright among men: they all lie in wait for blood; they hunt every man his brother with a net" (v.2). Evil was practised with earnestness and expertise: 'both hands are for evil, to do it well!' (v.3 JND). Micah might have been writing about crime in the twenty-first century!

- He had no confidence in state officers. Political life was affected. The officials did not "do justly" (6:8). "The prince asketh, and the judge asketh for a reward; and the great man, he uttereth his mischievous desire: so they wrap it up. The best of them is as a brier: the most upright is sharper than a thorn hedge" (vv.3-4). The word rendered, "wrap", means to 'weave' or 'twist'. Today we call it 'sleaze'. The words which follow ("The day of thy watchmen and thy visitation cometh; now shall be their perplexity") could refer to the true prophets: in which case, "The day of thy watchmen and thy visitation", refers to the predictions of the prophets, and the words, "now shall be their perplexity", refers to the corrupt state officers. They could however refer to the false prophets who had been false watchmen and were destined to utter confusion.

- He had no confidence in friends. Social life was affected; "Trust ye not in a friend, put ye not confidence in a guide" (v.5) or 'Believe ye not in a companion, put not confidence in a familiar friend' (JND). The Lord Jesus fully understood these circumstances. We can discern the "spirit of Christ" in David when he wrote, "Yea, mine own familiar friend, in whom I trusted, which did eat of my bread, hath lifted up his heel against me" (Psalm 41:9, cited in John 13:18).

- He had no confidence in family. Family life was affected: "Keep the doors of thy mouth from her that lieth in thy bosom. For the son dishonoureth the father, the daughter riseth up against her mother, the daughter in law against her mother in law; a man's enemies are the men of his own house" (vv.5-6). Compare Mark 13 verse 12, "Now the brother shall betray the brother to death, and the father the son: and children shall rise up against their parents, and shall cause them to be put to death". See Jeremiah 9 verse 4, "Take ye heed every one of his neighbour, and trust ye not in any brother: for every brother will utterly supplant, and every neighbour will walk with slanders".

The Lord Jesus refers to this passage in Matthew 10 verses 35-36 when speaking to His disciples about the divisive effect of the gospel. While we know that the gospel unites families, many of God's people know only too well that it can also divide families. W. Kelly observes that "nothing brings out the malice of the heart so much as the pressure of God's grace on men; nor does anything else expose a man to so much contempt and hatred". But the Lord is "as a little sanctuary" (Ezek. 11:16) and many of God's people have been able to exclaim, "When my father and my mother forsake me, then the LORD will take me up" (Psalm 27:10).

b) God is faithful, v.7

Although, humanly speaking, Micah had every reason for distress and despair, his lament in verses 1-6 gives place to triumphant faith in verse 7: "Therefore I will look unto the LORD; I will wait for the God of my salvation: my God will hear me" or "But ***as for me,*** I will look unto Jehovah ..." (JND). Like Isaiah, he says, "Cease ye from man, whose breath is in his nostrils: for wherein is he to be accounted of?" (Isa. 2:22). Micah's one and only resource is God Himself. The believer can cheerfully sing:

His oath, His covenant, and blood
Support me in the 'whelming flood:
When all around my soul gives way,
He then is all my hope and stay.

But it was far more than an empty technicality. We should notice the intimacy of Micah's relationship with God: "***my*** God will hear me". He evidently enjoyed God's personal presence and help. After all, this was the man who said, "But truly I am full of power by the spirit of the LORD, and of judgment, and of might, to declare unto Jacob his transgression, and to Israel his sin" (Micah 3:8). We should notice that Micah's relationship with God promoted:

i) Concentration of vision

"I will look unto the LORD." Micah had looked around him, and found nothing but discouragement and disappointment. Now he looks in a totally different direction, reminding us of the need to "run with patience the race that is set before us, looking unto Jesus the author and finisher of (our) faith" (Heb. 12:1-2). The supreme example is the Lord Jesus Himself who said, "I have set the LORD always before me" (Psalm 16:8).

ii) Continuance of hope

"I will wait for the God of my salvation." Micah believed that God would intervene in His own time and was prepared to wait for this to happen. The believers at Thessalonica were known for their "patience (endurance) of hope in our Lord Jesus Christ" (1 Thess. 1:3). We can reassure our hearts that "he that shall come will come, and will not tarry" (Heb. 10:37).

iii) Confidence in prayer

"My God will hear me." We must never forget the statement in Psalm 66 verse 18, "If I regard iniquity in my heart, the Lord will not hear me". The Psalmist evidently met that condition, for he continues, "But verily God ***hath*** heard me; he ***hath*** attended to the voice of my prayer". See 1 John 3 verse 22: "And whatsoever we ask, we receive of him, because we keep his commandments, and do those things that are pleasing in his sight", and 1 John 5 verse 14: "if we ask anything according to his will, he heareth us".

2) ISRAEL'S COMING CAPTIVITY, vv.8-10

While Micah speaks in the first person, he does so "as the representative of the godly remnant, in emphatic contrast to the sinful mass of the people" *(Unger's Commentary on the Old Testament)*. Notice here Micah's complete confidence in the faithfulness of God: "I shall … he will". The paragraph begins with the words, "Rejoice not against me, O mine enemy", and proceeds to give three reasons why the enemies of God's people would ultimately be confounded. Whilst, with Edom, they "rejoiced over the children of Judah in the day of their destruction" (Obad. v.12), that was not the end of the story. "Upon mount Zion shall be deliverance, and there shall be holiness; and the house of Jacob shall possess their possessions", (Obad. v.17). The enemy had no reason to rejoice because:

a) Israel's captivity is not permanent, v.8

"When I fall, I shall ***arise***; when I sit in darkness, the LORD shall be a ***light*** unto me." Paul refers to Israel's fall and rise in Romans 11 verses 11-15, "I say then, Have they stumbled that they should fall? God forbid: but rather through their fall salvation is come unto the Gentiles, for to provoke them to jealousy. Now if the fall of them be the riches of the world, and the diminishing of them the riches of the Gentiles; how much more their fulness?"

The words, "The LORD shall be a ***light*** unto me", recall Isaiah 60 verses 1-3, "Arise, shine; for thy light is come, and the glory of the LORD is risen upon thee. For, behold, the darkness shall cover the earth, and gross darkness the people: but the LORD shall arise upon thee, and his glory shall be seen upon thee. And the Gentiles shall come to thy light, and kings to the brightness of thy rising".

ii) Israel's affliction has a purpose, v.9

"I will bear the indignation of the LORD, because I have sinned against him, ***until*** he plead my cause, and execute judgment for me: he will bring me forth to the light, and I shall behold his righteousness." The Lord will not "plead" the cause of His people and "execute judgment" for them, until He has "washed away the filth of the daughters of Zion ... by the spirit of judgment, and by the spirit of burning" (Isa. 4:4). The nation is yet to pass through the unutterable horrors of the Great Tribulation, which will be "like a refiner's fire, and like fullers' soap" (Mal. 3:2).

iii) Israel's enemies will be punished, v.10

"Then she that is mine enemy shall see it, and shame shall cover her which said unto me, Where is the LORD thy God? mine eyes shall behold her: now shall she be trodden down as the mire of the streets." The ancient promise to Abraham will be completely fulfilled: "I will bless them that bless thee, ***and curse him that curseth thee"*** (Gen. 12:3).

3) ISRAEL'S CERTAIN REGATHERING, vv.11-17

This section explains and expands the words, "He will bring me forth to the light, and I shall behold his righteousness" (v.9). That is, God's righteousness in fulfilling the covenant. See verse 20, "Thou wilt perform the truth to Jacob, and the mercy to Abraham, which thou hast sworn to our fathers from the days of old". We should notice:

a) The rebuilding of the walls, v.11

"In the days that thy walls are to be built …" While the wall of Jerusalem was rebuilt under the guidance of Nehemiah, the prophecy looks far beyond the end of the Babylonian exile. See, for example, Isaiah 54 verse 11 ("I will lay thy stones with fair colours, and lay thy foundations with sapphires"); Isaiah

60 verse 11 ("And the sons of strangers shall build up thy walls"); Amos 9 verse 11 ("In that day will I raise up the tabernacle of David that is fallen ... and I will raise up his ruins, and I will build it as in days of old").

b) The removal of the decree, v.11

"In that day shall the decree be far removed" or "On that day shall the established limit recede" (JND). M.C. Unger states that the Hebrew is best rendered, "On that day will your boundary be extended". Compare Zechariah 10 verse 10: "I will bring them again also out of the land of Egypt, and gather them out of Assyria; and I will bring them into the land of Gilead and Lebanon; and place shall not be found for them".

c) The regathering of the nation, v.12

"In that day also he shall come even to thee from Assyria, and from the fortified cities, and from the fortress even to the river, and from sea to sea, and from mountain to mountain." But notice the parenthetical observation in verse 13, "Notwithstanding the land shall be desolate because of them that dwell therein, for the fruit of their doings". The ultimate resettlement of the land must not blind them to coming judgment.

d) The restoration of shepherd-care, v.14.

"Feed thy people with thy rod, the flock of thine heritage, which dwell solitarily in the wood, in the midst of Carmel: let them feed in Bashan and Gilead, as ***in the days of old.***" M.C. Unger comments as follows, "The millennial flock is pictured dwelling by itself in the woodland, in the midst of a fruitful field. No longer will the Shepherd's flock be scattered among the pagan nations, but they will dwell as distinct people in their own land". See Numbers 23 verse 9: "Lo, the people shall ***dwell alone***, and shall not be reckoned among the nations". Unger continues, "They not only will feed in the tranquil woodland pastures and fruitful field (Carmel), but also in Transjordan, in the superb pasturelands of Bashan and Gilead, as in the days of old, that is, in the time of David and Solomon". This points to the coming fulfillment for restored Israel in the Kingdom age of all God's promises concerning her prosperity. The nation will then have undisturbed enjoyment of the entire territory promised to Abraham and his posterity. See Genesis 15 verses 18-21.

e) The renewal of divine power, v.15

"According to the days of thy coming out of the land of Egypt will I shew unto him marvellous things." When Israel left Egypt, neither human animosity nor natural barriers thwarted the purpose of God. At the end-time, God will intervene when and where it is necessary to achieve the restoration and blessing of His people. Amongst other things, He will "utterly destroy the tongue of the Egyptian sea; and with his mighty wind shall he shake his hand over the river (Euphrates), and shall smite it in the (JND 'into') seven streams, and make men go over dryshod" (Isa. 11:15).

f) The reaction of the nations, vv.16-17

"The nations shall see and be confounded at all their might: they shall lay their hand upon their mouth (they will be speechless and ashamed of what they had said previously, see v.10), their ears shall be deaf (perhaps meaning that they will "close their ears in order not to hear of Israel's successes", M.C. Unger). They shall lick the dust like a serpent, they shall move out of their holes like worms of the earth: they shall be afraid of the LORD our God, and shall fear because of thee." In that day, Israel will be "the head, and not the tail" of the nations (Deut. 28:13), and say, with David, "Thou hast given me the necks of mine enemies" (Psalm 18:40).

4) GOD'S COVENANT MERCY, vv.18-20

In the closing verses of the prophecy, we learn that God will act in grace and lovingkindness towards His people on account of the patriarchal covenant. We should notice the following:

a) He will reveal His love, v.18

"Who is a God like unto thee, that pardoneth iniquity, and passeth by the transgression of the remnant of his heritage? he retaineth not his anger for ever, because he delighteth in mercy." The final words can be translated, 'He delighteth in ***loving-kindness***' (JND). Unlike Jonah, Micah rejoiced in God's mercy. Jonah would have rejoiced if God had executed judgment on Nineveh! We must remember that the God who delights to show mercy requires His people to do the same: see Micah 6 verse 8. He has been merciful to us: see Hebrews 8 verse 12. We are to forgive one another in the same way that God has forgiven us (Eph. 4:32).

We must remember that the basis on which God can rightly pass by "the transgression of the remnant of his heritage" is the death of Christ. This is clear from Romans 3 verses 25-26, "Being justified freely by his grace through the redemption that is in Christ Jesus: whom God hath set forth (to be) a propitiation through faith in his blood, to declare his righteousness for the remission (passing over) of ***sins that are past***, through the forebearance of God". We must always remember that the efficacy of the work of Christ at Calvary extended backward through time, as well as forward. We must not forget either that whilst the Old Testament sacrifices had no intrinsic value, they certainly had an extrinsic value. By offering the appropriate sacrifice, the Israelite put himself in a position to benefit from the death of Christ, even though that great work was not accomplished at the time. Men and women have only been, and will only be justified on the basis of His finished work at Calvary. Israel's ultimate salvation and blessing rests on exactly the same basis as our own.

No wonder that Micah could exclaim, "Who is a God like unto thee!" These words first occur in Exodus 15 verse 11, "Who is like unto thee, O LORD, among the gods? Who is like thee, glorious in holiness, fearful in praises, doing wonders?" God is incomparable!

b) He will remove their sins, v.19

"He will turn again, he will have compassion on us; he will subdue our iniquities; and thou wilt cast all their sins into the depths of the sea." Notice the change from "us" to "their." The remnant will be "all righteous" (Isaiah 60:21). Other prophets contribute to the theme: "I will also leave in the midst of thee an afflicted and poor people, and they shall trust in the name of the LORD. The remnant of Israel shall not do iniquity, nor speak lies ... Be glad and rejoice with all the heart, O daughter of Jerusalem. The LORD hath taken away thy judgments" (Zeph. 3:12-15). "In those days, and in that time, saith the LORD, the iniquity of Israel shall be sought for, and there shall be none; and the sins of Judah, and they shall not be found: for I will pardon them whom I reserve (JND, 'whom I leave remaining')" (Jer. 50:20). "Then will I sprinkle clean water upon you, and ye shall be clean: from all your filthiness, and from all your idols, will I cleanse you" (Ezek. 36:25).

It has often been pointed out that the place into which Israel's sins will be cast is the very place where the Saviour suffered for sins. Israel's sins will be "cast ... into the depths of the sea" (see addendum), and the Lord Jesus cried under divine judgment, “All thy waves and thy billows are gone over me” (Psalm 42:7). The ‘greater than Jonah’ cried, in effect, “For thou hadst cast me into the deep, ***in the midst of the seas;*** and thy floods compassed me about: all thy billows and thy waves passed over me” (Jonah 2:3).

c) He will ratify the covenant, v.20

“Thou wilt perform the truth to Jacob, and the mercy to Abraham, which thou hast sworn unto our fathers from the days of old.” It is interesting to notice that the passage in which God describes His love for Israel continues with reference to His promises to the patriarchs. Moses told Israel that the Lord loved them and chose them ***(i)*** “because the LORD loved you” and ***(ii)*** “because he would keep the oath which he had sworn unto your fathers” (Deut. 7:8). We must not forget that the promises made to patriarchs were unconditional. While Israel lost the joy of her inheritance and relationship with God through disobedience and unbelief, “Lo-ammi” (meaning, ‘not my people’) is not for ever, for “in the place where it was said unto them, Ye are not my people, there it shall be said unto them, Ye are the sons of the living God” (Hos. 1:8-11). Every promise of God, whatever its scope and subject, will be fulfilled in Christ, for “all the promises of God in him are yea, and in him Amen, unto the glory of God” (2 Cor. 1:20).

The chapter begins with Micah’s misery over human failure, and ends with his joy over God’s faithfulness, reminding us of Psalm 115 verse 1, “Not unto us, O LORD, not unto us, but unto thy name give glory, for thy ***mercy***, and for thy ***truth’s*** sake”. We can sing ***now*** what Israel will most certainly sing in the future as they contemplate the grace and loving-kindness of God:

Great God of wonder! all Thy ways
Display the attributes divine;
But countless acts of pardoning grace
Beyond Thine other wonders shine:
Who is a pardoning God like Thee?
Or who has grace so rich and free?

Addendum

“Thou wilt cast all their sins into the depths of the sea.” The late Fred Elliott was travelling across the North Pacific Ocean when his attention was drawn by a ship’s officer to the fact that the vessel was passing over the Mariana

Trench, the deepest part of the world oceans. The Challenger Deep at the southern end of the Mariana Trench is 10,920 metres deep – approximately 6 ¾ miles. Having heard this from the ship's officer, Mr. Elliott exclaimed, "Praise the Lord", and then explained to him the reason: 'God has cast all ***my*** sins into the depths of the sea!'

NAHUM

by

John M Riddle

NAHUM

1) Introduction

The Subject of the Book

The books of Jonah and Nahum are both concerned with the city of Nineveh and, therefore, with the affairs of the Assyrian Empire. This serves to remind us that whilst the bulk of Old Testament prophecy concerns Israel and Judah, God takes an intense interest in the surrounding nations. Whilst the ministry of Jonah, Nahum and Obadiah was specifically concerned with Gentile nations, considerable space is allocated to the nations in other prophetic books. See, for example, Isaiah 13-23 and Amos 1-2. God deals with the nations in connection with their treatment of His people. This is made very clear as early as Genesis 12 verse 3, “I will bless them that bless thee, and curse him that curseth thee: and in thee shall all families of the earth be blessed”. Compare Zechariah 2 verse 8, “He that toucheth you toucheth the apple of his eye”. We should not think that this applies only to Israel’s immediate neighbours in the Middle East, although for obvious reasons they are largely prominent. The whole world is involved with the Jew to a smaller or larger extent. Listen to Zechariah again: “Behold, the day of the LORD cometh, and thy spoil shall be divided in the midst of thee. For I will gather ***all nations*** against Jerusalem to battle ... and it shall come to pass, that every one that is left of all the nations which came against Jerusalem shall even go up from year to year to worship the King” (14:1-2, 16).

The divine attributes given in Romans 11 verse 22 apply to the books of Jonah and Nahum respectively. Over the book of ***Jonah***, we could write, ***‘Behold the goodness of God’***. Over the book of ***Nahum,*** we could write ***‘Behold the severity of God’***. By linking the two books in this way, we are reminded that God’s mercy is not a permanent institution. “My Spirit shall not always strive with men.”

The books of Jonah and Nahum contrast in another way. We know a great deal about Jonah personally, but very little about his preaching. In fact, the message of the book surrounds the man himself. On the other hand, we know practically nothing about Nahum personally, but we do have an extensive record of his preaching. One thing is very clear: Jonah would have said a hearty 'Amen' to Nahum's preaching. It was just what he wanted to hear!

The Date of the Book

It is possible to place an approximate date on the prophecy of Nahum by reference to the fall of Thebes ("Populous No", 3:8-10), and the fall of Nineveh itself. "No" or "No-amon" was the ancient Egyptian name for Thebes. It was overthrown in 663 B.C. by the Assyrians under Ashurbanipal. Nineveh fell to the Medo-Babylonian army in 612 B.C. The prophecy of Nahum must, therefore, be dated between these two events.

This is very interesting from another point of view. The dates given above take us to the era of Josiah's reign. Whilst the power of Assyria was declining, it still posed a threat to Judah, see 2 Kings 23 verse 29. It seems, therefore, highly significant that God announced judgment on the enemy when His people had turned to Him and renounced idolatry. We should note the lesson.

The Structure of the Book

The prophecy of Nahum can be divided by the chapter divisions as follows: ***Chapter 1***, The Executor of Judgment on Nineveh; ***Chapter 2***, The Execution of Judgment on Nineveh; ***Chapter 3***, The Explanation of Judgment on Nineveh. Alternatively: ***Chapter 1***, Judgment Declared; ***Chapter 2***, Judgment Described; ***Chapter 3***, Judgment Deserved. Every Bible student makes his, or her, own analysis with titles to match.

The Introduction to the Book

"The burden of Nineveh. The book of the vision of Nahum the Elkoshite", (Chapter 1:1). We must notice at least three things in this introduction:

1) It is "the burden of ***Nineveh***". The Assyrians were a constant threat to Israel and Judah. They had, of course, been responsible for the destruction of the northern kingdom years before Nahum's prophecy. See 2 Kings 17 for a detailed record of Israel's final conquest by Shalmaneser. This prompted the Assyrians, under Sennacherib, to attack Judah during the reign of

Hezekiah. The invasion proved disastrous: the Assyrians lost 185,000 men in one night, and Sennacherib himself was assassinated by his two sons on his return to Nineveh. See 2 Kings 18-19. The Assyrians returned to Judah during the reign of Hezekiah's son, Manasseh, but evidently not for long (see 2 Chronicles 33:11-13), and we have already noticed their connection with Josiah. But this isn't the end of the story. ***Assyria has a future role.***

Micah 5 verses 2-6 describes the coming "Ruler in Israel; whose goings forth have been from of old, from everlasting". The passage emphasises His delivering power: "He shall stand and feed in the strength of the LORD, in the majesty of the name of the LORD his God ... and this man shall be the peace: ***when the Assyrian shall come into our land*** ... and they shall waste the ***land of Assryia*** with the sword ... thus shall he deliver us from ***the Assyrian***, when he cometh into our land, and when he treadeth within our borders". Prophetic students are not altogether agreed on the identity of the future Assyrian! It might be worth remembering that much of the ancient Assyrian Empire lay within territory now occupied by modern Iraq and Iran. On the other hand, it included territory occupied until recently by the former U.S.S.R., which could direct us to Ezekiel 38-39. After all, God does say, "Art thou he of whom I have spoken in old time by my servants the prophets of Israel, which prophesied in those days many years that I would bring thee against them?" (Ezek. 38:17). But we look in vain for other references to Gog and his colleagues in the Old Testament. Yet God tells us that His prophets have spoken about him! We should also bear in mind that Isaiah 10, which describes a past Assyrian invasion, suddenly gives place to Isaiah 11-12, which describes the future reign of Christ. The connection between past and future lies in the fact that the past invasion prefigures a future invasion from the same area. Scripture views the invader as the same power and, therefore, shows the ultimate and final defeat of that power, without reference to the intervening centuries. We have another example in Daniel 9 verse 26.

2) It is, "The ***burden*** of Nineveh. The book of the ***vision*** of Nahum". The Holy Spirit brings the two words together for a purpose. Nahum's vision became Nahum's burden. We have something similar in the New Testament: "Then spake the Lord to Paul in the night by a vision, Be not afraid, but speak, and hold not thy peace: for I am with thee, and no man shall set on thee to hurt thee: for I have much people in this city. And he continued there a year and six months, teaching the word of God among them" (Acts 18:9-10). How much do ***we*** feel the weight of the things God reveals to us in His word?

3) It is, "The book of the vision of ***Nahum,*** the Elkoshite". Elkosh remains unidentified, and we should perhaps avoid making too much of the fact that Capernaum means 'city of Nahum'! But Nahum does mean 'comfort' or 'consolation', which reminds us that we have a similar man in the New Testament. Barnabas means, 'son of consolation' or 'exhortation'. Nahum's message of consolation is contained in Chapter 1 verse 15, "Behold upon the mountains the feet of him that bringeth good tidings, that publisheth peace!" The "good tidings" were, of course, the news that Nineveh was overthrown. This does not necessarily mean that the city had actually fallen at the time of writing, but that its fall was certain. We have the consolation of knowing that there will be "great voices in heaven, saying, The kingdoms of this world are become the kingdom of our Lord, and of his Christ; and he shall reign for ever and ever" (Rev. 11:15). The word "Nahum" appears in Chapter 3 verse 7, "Whence shall I seek ***comforters*** for thee?" But there was no "Nahum" for the Lord Jesus: see Psalm 69 verse 20, "I looked for some to take pity, but there was none; and for ***comforters,*** but I found none".

ADDENDUM

We are told that Nineveh was apparently impregnable. Its walls were one hundred feet high, and broad enough for three chariots to drive abreast along them. Its circumference was sixty miles, adorned with 1,200 towers. It had fifteen gates and enclosed 1,800 acres. Sennacherib gave Nineveh its renown: he not only created a palace and an arena, but laid out a park in which he accumulated exotic animals and plants.

NAHUM

2) The Executor of Judgment on **Nineveh**

Read Chapter 1:1-6

In introducing Nahum, we noticed that the prophecy can be divided by the chapter divisions as follows: ***Chapter 1***, The Executor of Judgment on Nineveh; ***Chapter 2***, The Execution of Judgment on Nineveh; ***Chapter 3***, the Explanation of Judgment on Nineveh. Chapter 1 describes the character of God as the Judge of Nineveh in two ways: first, in relation to the oppressor (vv.1-6) and, second, in relation to the oppressed (vv.7-15).

We will highlight some of the statements in each section of this chapter, rather than attempting a verse-by-verse commentary.

1) God's character in dealing with the oppressor, vv.1-6

It is worth noticing that it is not our business to seek any form of revenge on those who oppose us. That is God's prerogative. "Dearly beloved, avenge not yourselves, but rather give place unto wrath (of God): for it is written, Vengeance is mine, I will repay, saith the Lord" (Romans 12:19). See also 2 Thessalonians 1 verses 6-7: "Seeing it is a righteous thing with God to recompense tribulation to them that trouble you".

In this connection, we should notice:

a) The Jealousy of God, v.2

"God is jealous, and the LORD revengeth." We should notice that the Scriptures refer to at least three aspects of the jealousy of God:

- ***He is jealous of His own glory.*** See, for example, Ezekiel 39 verse 25 ("I ... will be jealous for my holy name") and Isaiah 48 verse 11 ("I will not give my glory unto another"). The demise of Dagon illustrates the point. We must never forget that God is unchanging. Paul was obliged to remind the proud saints at Corinth that their past should remind them "that no flesh should glory in his presence", and that their rich blessings in Christ should remind them that "he that glorieth, let him glory in the Lord" (1 Cor. 1:26-31).

- ***He is jealous of the affections of His people.*** "I the LORD thy God am a jealous God" (Exodus 20:5). This statement is a warning against idolatry: "Thou shalt have no other gods before me" (Exodus 20:3). See also Exodus 34 verse 14, "Thou shalt worship no other god: for the LORD, whose name is Jealous, is a jealous God" (Exodus 34:14). He has every right to our complete love and devotion, first of all, because He is ***God,*** and, secondly, because of all that He has done for us in Christ. Have **we** left our "first love"?

- ***He is jealous for His people.*** It is to this that Nahum refers. They had been wronged, and God intervenes on their behalf. Compare Joel 2 verse 18 and Zechariah 1 verse 14. We must remember that God is still jealous for His people Israel. It is still true that "he that toucheth you toucheth the apple of his eye" (Zech. 2:8). We too should be jealous for God's people: that is, deeply concerned when their spiritual welfare is threatened. Paul expressed his "godly jealousy" in 2 Corinthians 11 verse 2: "I am jealous over you with godly jealousy: for I have espoused you to one husband, that I may present you as a chaste virgin to Christ". Hence his condemnation of the false teachers who had invaded the assembly at Corinth.

b) The Vengeance of God, v.2

"The LORD revengeth, and is furious; the LORD ***will*** take vengeance on his adversaries, and he reserveth wrath for his enemies." There is, of course, a difference between 'revenge' (retribution) and 'avenge' (retribution). Hence the New Translation (JND) reads: "an avenger is Jehovah, and full of fury". God's intention to avenge the cruel treatment of His people flows from His jealousy for them. The Assyrians had afflicted God's beloved people and had, therefore, caused distress to God Himself. We should notice that Nahum does not say that He will have vengeance on the adversaries of His people, but "on ***His*** adversaries".

c) The Longsuffering of God, v.3

"The LORD is slow to anger." Isaiah tells us that judgment is God's "strange work ... his strange act" (Isa. 28:21). Many years had passed since Jonah went to Nineveh. During that time, Assyria had oppressed both northern and southern kingdoms, and had done so in the face of severe warnings. But now, like the Amorites before them (Gen. 15:16), the iniquity of Nineveh was "full". The longsuffering of God which "waited in the days of Noah" (1 Pet. 3:20), is still operative. He is "longsuffering to us-ward, not willing that any should perish, but that all should come to repentance" (2 Pet. 3:9). Little do men and women know that He delays intervention in world affairs for their good. Compare Exodus 34 verses 6-7.

d) The Justice of God, v.3

"The LORD … will not at all acquit the wicked." We must never think that evil men and women will escape unscathed. The Psalmist discovered that appearances can be deceptive. "I was envious at the foolish, when I saw the prosperity of the wicked. For there are no bands in their death" (Psalm 73:3-4). He found the solution to his problem in the presence of God: "When I thought to know this, it was too painful for me; until I went into the sanctuary of God; then understood I their end" (vv.16-17). The longsuffering of God is not at variance with His justice. He "hath appointed a day, in the which he ***will*** judge the world in righteousness by that man whom he hath ordained" (Acts 17:31). Peter reminds us that "the day of the Lord ***will*** come as a thief in the night" (2 Peter 3:10). God will have the last word in human history.

It will not go amiss to be reminded that as the Lord's people, "we must all appear before the judgment seat of Christ; that every one may receive the things done in his body, according to that he hath done, whether it be good or bad" (2 Cor. 5:10).

e) The Power of God, v.3

"The LORD is ... great in power." He is perfectly able to implement His justice, and the balance of the section proves the point. "The Lord hath his way in the whirlwind and in the storm …" (vv.3-6). His power is irresistible. The rich pastures of Bashan, the vineyards of Carmel, and the forests of Lebanon, all wither "before the searing blast of the divine anger" (M. C. Unger). Nothing can stand before His power. The Creator uses the mighty forces of storm, earthquake and volcanic eruption to secure His purposes. The world is yet to experience the full hostility of nature under divine direction. See, for example, Isaiah 24 verse 20 and Revelation 6 verses 12-17. But we must also remember that God uses men and nations to accomplish His purposes. The Assyrians themselves once fulfilled this role: “O Assyrian, the rod of mine anger, and the staff in their hand is mine indignation” (Isa. 10:5).

In the second section of the chapter (vv.7-15), Nahum describes the character of God in connection with His oppressed people.

NAHUM

3) The Executor of Judgment on Nineveh (Continued)

Read Chapter 1:7-15

Nahum 1 describes the Executor of judgment of Nineveh in two ways: ***(i)*** His character in dealing with the oppressor (vv.1-6), and ***(ii)*** His character in delivering the oppressed (vv.7-15). We have already considered the first of these, and noticed the Jealousy of God (v.2), the Vengeance of God (v.2), the Longsuffering of God (v.3), the Justice of God (v.3), and the Power of God (vv.3-6). This brings us to -

2) His character in delivering the oppressed, vv.7-15

In this connection, we should notice the following:

a) The Goodness of God, v.7

"The LORD is good, a stronghold in the day of trouble; and he knoweth them that trust in him." God is able to protect His people, even against such an immensely powerful enemy as Assyria. There are at least three things to note in this verse:

- ***"The LORD is good."*** He is good in every way. See, for example, Psalm 107 verse 1, "O give thanks unto the LORD, for He is ***good"***; Psalm 69 verse 16, "Thy lovingkindness is ***good***"; Psalm 143 verse 10, "Teach me to do thy will; for thou art my God: thy Spirit is ***good***". The Lord Jesus said, "I am the ***good*** (*kalos*: intrinsically good) Shepherd" (John 10:11). He was addressed as, "***Good (****agathos:* beneficial in effect) Master" (Matt. 19:16).

- ***"The LORD is ... a stronghold in the day of trouble."*** David put it like this: "But the salvation of the righteous is of the LORD: He is their strength in the time of trouble, and the Lord shall help them and deliver them: He shall deliver them from the wicked, and save them, because they trust in him" (Psalm 37:39-40). We too have a "stronghold in the day of trouble": see Hebrews 4 verse 16, "Let us therefore come boldly unto the throne of grace, that we may obtain mercy, and find grace to help ***in time of need***".

Assyrian strongholds are described as "fig trees with the firstripe figs: if they be shaken, they shall even fall into the mouth of the eater" (Nahum 3:12). That's how easily their strongholds would fall! Not so our divine stronghold. Everything there inspires confidence. "The eternal God is thy refuge, and underneath are the everlasting arms" (Deut. 33:27); "A glorious high throne from the beginning is the place of our sanctuary" (Jer. 17:12)!

- ***"The LORD ... knoweth them that trust in him."*** (Note: the words in 2 Tim. 2:19, "The Lord knoweth them that are his", cite Numbers 16:5 rather than Nahum 1:7, which is more than a statement of divine omniscience.) We can, of course, take these lovely words exactly as they stand. He knows that we do trust in Him. But they also emphasise that God acknowledges "them that trust in him". This is confirmed by the words following: "But with an overunning flood he will make an utter end of the place thereof, and darkness shall pursue his enemies" (v.8). The passage recognises only two classes of people: "them that trust in him", and "his enemies". There is no middle ground. (Compare Matt. 12:30.) We know that our relationship with God is far more than a technical nicety: there is warmth and intimacy. The Song of Solomon expresses it beautifully: "My beloved is mine, and I am his ... I am my beloved's, and my beloved is mine ... I am my beloved's, and his desire is towards me" (Song of Solomon 2:16; 6:3; 7:10).

A few explanatory notes might be helpful in connection with verses 8-11. Further help can be obtained from more detailed commentaries.

- The reference to ***"an overunning flood"*** (v.8) is evidently more than poetical language. To quote Hobart E. Freeman (*Nahum. Zephaniah, Habakkuk. Minor Prophets of the Seventh Century B.C.*, p.20), "Archeological records seem to indicate that a vital part of the walls of Nineveh was destroyed by an unusually heavy flood of the Tigris River, thus permitting the enemy to force its way through this breach and storm the city".

- The words, "He will make an ***utter*** end (see also vv.8, 15): affliction shall not rise up ***the second time***" (v.9), are best explained by the fact that whilst the Assyrians were permitted to capture and deport Israel in the north, they would not be allowed to do so with Judah.

- The words, "For while they be folden together as thorns, and while they are ***drunken as drunkards***, they shall be devoured as stubble fully dry" (v.10), refer to the fact that the Assyrians thought their city was invincible and "gave themselves to excessive drinking and revelry" (H. E. Freeman, as above, p.21). The historian, Diodorus Siculus, refers to "the drunken revelries of the king and his courtiers during the siege of the capital" (Quoted in *Unger's Commentary on the Old Testament*, p.1883).

- The "one come out of thee, that imagineth evil against the LORD, a ***wicked counsellor***" (v.11), is undoubtedly Sennacherib whose emissary Rab-shakeh said, "Who are they among all the gods of the countries, that have delivered their country out of mine hand, that the LORD should deliver Jerusalem out of mine hand?" (2 Kings 18:27-35). More of the same followed: this time in a letter; "Let not thy God in whom thou trustest deceive thee, saying, Jerusalem shall not be delivered into the hand of the king of Assyria" (19:8-13).

b) The Deliverance of God, vv.12-14

"Thus saith the LORD; Though they be quiet (meaning 'unscathed, whole, complete, at full strength', M.C.Unger, as above, p.1884), and likewise many, yet thus shall they be cut down, when he shall pass through ('pass away', RV/JND). Though I have afflicted thee, I will afflict thee no more. For now will I break his yoke from off thee, and will burst thy bonds in sunder." As it stands, in the future tense, the entire passage refers to the coming destruction of Nineveh. H. E. Freeman (as above p.21) observes, however, that the verbs in verses 11-12 indicate something that is past or completed, so that we should read: 'Thus saith the LORD: Though they were at full strength, and likewise many, even so they have been cut down, and he has passed away'. This can only refer to the destruction of Sennecharib's army, and the death of Sennacherib himself. (See 2 Kings 19:35-37.) The Assyrian army was defeated by divine power, and now the empire itself was to fall. Even after the loss of 185,000 men, and the death of the king, Assyria remained a threat to Judah. But now God says, "Though I have afflicted thee, I will afflict thee no more. For ***now*** will I break his yoke from off thee, and will burst thy bonds in sunder".

It is worth pondering the words, ***"Though I have afflicted thee, I will afflict thee no more"***. This generates two questions:

i) Why does God say, "I have afflicted thee"?

Why did God allow the Assyrians to invade Palestine? Quite evidently, He had no difficulty in removing them, but why let them come in the first place? The answer lies in Isaiah 10: "O Assyrian, the rod of mine anger, and the staff in their hand is mine indignation. I will send him against an hypocritical nation, and against the people of my wrath will I give him a charge" (vv.5-6). The Assyrians were used by God to discipline His people, but we must not think that God then discarded them purely because they had served His purpose. Continue to read Isaiah 10!

What about ourselves? Think about the defeat at Ai in Joshua 7. Defeat at enemy hands highlighted the fact that something was wrong. God was not prepared to give His people victory until they had dealt with Achan. Years later, Solomon prayed: "And if thy people Israel be put to the worse before the enemy, because they have sinned against thee; and shall return and confess thy name, and pray and make supplication before thee in this house; then hear thou from the heavens …" To which God replied, "If my people, which are called by my name, shall humble themselves, and pray, and seek my face, and turn from their wicked ways; then will I hear from heaven, and will forgive their sin, and will heal their land" (2 Chron. 6:24-25; 7:14). Are we suffering constant defeat? There can only be one reason, and only one remedy. The prodigal son, brought to his senses by absolute penury, said, "I will arise and go to my father, and will say unto him, Father, I have sinned against heaven, and before thee" (Luke 15:18). We should notice the order: "I have sinned against ***heaven***, and before thee".

ii) Why does God say, "I will afflict thee no more"?

Isaiah 10 explains: "Wherefore it shall come to pass, that ***when the Lord hath performed his whole work upon mount Zion and on Jerusalem,*** I will punish the fruit of the stout heart of the king of Assyria, and the glory of his high looks", (v.12). What was His "whole work upon mount Zion"? Certainly not annihilation. Hezekiah turned to God, and now, if we've got our dates right, the great revival in Josiah's reign was beginning. Conditions now existed which enabled God to bless and deliver His people.

Once again, an explanatory note or two might be helpful - this time in connection with verse 14:

- "Out of the house of thy gods will I cut off the graven image and the molten image." This was the precise boast of Rab-shakeh: "Hath any of the gods of the nations delivered at all his land out of the hand of the king of Assyria? Where are the gods of Hamath, and of Arpad? Where are the gods of Sepharvaim, Hena and Ivah?" (2 Kings 18:33-34).

- "I will make thy grave; for thou art vile." The meaning is very clear: Nineveh would be buried. It was buried very successfully, which isn't surprising: God always does a good job! Every trace of Nineveh's existence disappeared for over two thousand years. The besieging army pillaged the city, and then burnt it to the ground. They razed its houses, temples, palaces, and fortifications to the extent that even its actual site was unknown, so much so that Bible critics were sceptical about references to the city. It was only in 1845, when Layard identified the site known as Kuyunjik as the ancient city of Nineveh, that the grave was discovered. Let's simply make the point that God's word is accurate to the finest detail, and His figures of speech are perfect.

But there is something to add: Ezekiel is commanded to "wail for the multitude of Egypt, and cast them down, even her, and the daughters of the famous nations, unto the nether parts of the earth, with them that go down to the pit", (Ezek. 32:17-18). The passage continues: "Asshur is there and all her company: his graves are about him: all of them slain, fallen by the sword; whose graves are set in the sides of the pit, and her company is round about her grave: all of them slain, fallen by the sword, which caused terror in the land of the living" (Ezek. 32:22-23).

c) The message from God, v.15

"Behold upon the mountains the feet of him that bringeth good tidings, that publisheth peace! O Judah, keep thy solemn feasts, perform thy vows: for the wicked shall no more pass through thee; he is utterly cut off." As we noticed in introduction, it is just here that the prophet's name is displayed – 'consolation'. The capital of Assyria had fallen, and there was peace at last. Similar words are found in Isaiah 52: "How beautiful upon the mountains are the feet of him that bringeth good tidings, that publisheth peace; that bringeth tidings of good, that publisheth salvation; that saith unto Zion, Thy God reigneth" (v.7). Nahum appears to be quoting Isaiah! This passage refers to the coming glory of Jerusalem: "Awake, awake; put on thy strength, O Zion; put on thy beautiful garments, O Jerusalem, the holy city" (Isa. 52:1). The reason for such glory is explained: the once-rejected Messiah will be "exalted and extolled, and be very high" (Isa. 52:13). But do notice that the "good tidings" in Isaiah 52 follow oppression: "My people went down aforetime into Egypt to sojourn there; and ***the Assyrian oppressed them without cause***" (Isa. 52:4).

Paul refers to these Old Testament passages in Romans 10: "And how shall they preach, except they be sent? As it is written, How beautiful are the feet of them that preach the gospel of peace, and bring glad tidings of good things!" (v.15). We too have "good tidings". An enemy has been defeated, and there is peace. The Lord Jesus has died that "through death he might destroy him that had the power of death, that is, the devil; and deliver them who through fear of death were all their lifetime subject to bondage" (Heb. 2:14-15). But what was Judah free to do? Not free to please themselves, but free to "keep thy solemn feasts, perform thy vows" (v.15). The "solemn feasts" were, of course, the "feasts of the LORD". See Leviticus 23. However, the word "solemn" doesn't quite hit the right note here. The Hebrew *chag* really means 'festival', hence the translation, "Celebrate thy feasts, Judah" (JND). This speaks for itself!

NAHUM

4) The Execution of Judgment on Nineveh

Read Chapter 2:1-5

Nahum 1 ***announces*** the destruction of Nineveh, and Nahum 2 ***describes*** the destruction of Nineveh. We must notice two general lessons in Chapter 2 before examining the detail.

- ***The chapter commences and concludes with reference to God.*** "He that dasheth in pieces is come up before thy face: keep the munition (fortress), watch the way, make thy loins strong, fortify the power mightily. For the ***LORD*** hath turned away ('brought again', JND: see also RV) the excellency of Jacob as the excellency of Israel" (vv.1-2). "Behold, I am against thee, saith the ***LORD of hosts***" (v.13). So Nineveh was to be destroyed by divine decree. There is no such thing as 'blind fate', or 'the fortunes of war'. God is in control of all world affairs, including its warfare. 1 Kings 22 is compulsory reading on this subject. Notice verses 19-22 particularly. The court of heaven is in session under the presidency of the Lord Himself. (See also Daniel 4:32; Job 1:6, 2:1; John 19:11.)

The latter part of the chapter emphasises the fact that God acts in perfect righteousness. This will become even more obvious when we reach the third chapter, but notice for now that when divine judgment falls, it is always deserved. See Amos 1-2, with the repeated phrase, "For three transgressions … and for four".

- ***The chapter describes the destruction of Nineveh in detail.*** For example, the uniforms of the soldiers are described: "the valiant men are in scarlet" (v.3). The movements of the chariots are strikingly depicted in verses 3-4. We will see more of this later. The very attention to detail emphasises the accuracy and certainty of Bible prophecy. This isn't in the least surprising. After all, "Holy men of God spake as they were moved by the Holy Ghost" (2 Pet. 1:21). God's word is clear and precise. It does not lend itself to human manipulation.

We must now give some thought to the detail in the chapter. As we have said, it describes the destruction of Nineveh. The chapter gives us the sequence of events.

1) THE CITY BESIEGED, vv.1-2

"He that dasheth in pieces is come up before thy face." History tells us that Nineveh was destroyed by an alliance of the Medes, Babylonians and Cythians under the command of Cyaxares and Nabopolassar. God describes the Babylonians as "the hammer of the whole earth" (Jeremiah 50:23), and continues by saying, "Thou art ***my battle axe*** and weapons of war: for with thee I will break in pieces the nations" (Jer. 51:20-26). This emphasises our first general point: God is in control of all world affairs.

With the besieging army at the gates of the city, Nineveh is urged to make herself as strong as possible: "Keep the munition (fortress), watch the way (keep a sharp lookout: the enemy might attack from any direction), make thy loins strong, fortify thy power mightily". As the chapter makes clear, they could make themselves as strong as they like, but it would all be in vain. The reason follows: "For the LORD hath turned away ('brought again', JND) the excellency of Jacob, as the excellency of Israel: for the emptiers have emptied them out, and marred their vine branches". It is helpful to read this verse in the New Translation (JND): "For Jehovah hath brought again the glory of Jacob, as the glory of Israel; for the wasters have wasted them, and marred their vine-branches". The Revised Version agrees with this rendering. The reference to Jacob and Israel is not to the southern and northern kingdoms, but to the nation generally. See Romans 11 verse 26, where both names are used for God's people in their entirety. These words are best understood with reference to Nahum 1 verse 12-13, "Though I have afflicted thee, I will afflict thee no more. For now will I break his yoke from off thee, and will burst thy bonds in sunder". Assyria 'emptied out', or 'wasted', God's people and "marred their vine branches". The expressions "glory of Jacob" and "glory of Israel", evidently refer, bearing in mind the context of the passage, to the restoration under King Josiah. There are two important things to notice:

- ***Israel is decribed as a vine.*** "Marred their ***vine branches***." See Isaiah

5 verses 1-7: "For the vineyard of the LORD of hosts is the house of Israel, and the men of Judah his pleasant plant". But there had been no fruit for God: in fact the vine had "brought forth wild grapes". But divine chastening by the hand of the Assyrian had purged the vine, and there was now fruit for God. We are immediately reminded of the Lord's teaching in John 15 verses 1-6. Bearing in mind the Old Testament parable of the vineyard, we do well to ask ourselves the question, "Are we producing 'wild grapes'?" (Isa. 5:2).

- Israel is delivered from oppression. God used the Assyrians to chasten His people, but their immense cruelty and pride brought them under divine judgment. It is helpful to read Isaiah 54 here. Notice the words, "No weapon that is formed against thee shall prosper" (v.17). The destruction of Nineveh is directly related to its activities against Israel. This is why the little word "for" connects verses 1-2: "He that dasheth in pieces is come up before thy face: keep the munition (fortress), watch the way, make thy loins strong, fortify thy power mightily. ***For*** the LORD hath turned away (brought again) the excellency of Jacob". See Zechariah 2 verse 8, "He that toucheth you toucheth the apple of his eye".

2) THE CITY ATTACKED, vv.3-5

We should notice reference to:

a) The attacking army, vv.3-4

Nahum describes ***the soldiers:*** "The shield of his mighty men is made red, the valiant men are in scarlet". We know from Isaiah 63 verses 1-6 that the colour red, for obvious reasons, is an emblem of judgment. So the language here could be figurative. On the other hand, it was customary to dye leather shields red in order to terrify the enemy. We are also told that scarlet (or 'vermillion') was a common colour for military and battle dress. It was certainly the colour of Chaldean uniforms: see Ezekiel 23 verse 14.

Nahum describes ***the chariots.*** "The chariots shall be with flaming torches in the day of his preparation." That is, the preparation by the commanding officers for attack. The NIV renders this: 'The metal on the chariots flashes'. The description of the chariots continues in verse 4, where the words "streets" and "broad ways" (open spaces) probably refer to the area surrounding the actual city itself.

Nahum describes ***the weapons.*** "The fir trees shall be terribly shaken." This probably refers to the spears and lances which were made of cypress wood.

b) The defending army, v.5

"He shall recount his worthies: they shall stumble in their walk; they shall make haste to the wall thereof, and the defence shall be prepared." It is only fair to say that not everybody assigns this verse to the defenders: some connect it with the attackers, and others partly to both. However, the words, "they shall stumble in their walk", seem more appropriate to the fearful and uncertain defenders, than to the powerful attackers. The words, "he shall recount his worthies", or 'he remembers his nobles', evidently refers to the command to man the defences of the city.

There was a time when the Assyrian nobles swept forward triumphantly. Now they "stumble" in their walk. Past achievements are now meaningless. It's a rather pathetic picture, isn't it?

But what about us? Are we 'stumbling in our walk'? Paul was obliged to say to the Galatians, "Ye did run well" (Gal. 5:7). We must listen to Solomon: "I have taught thee in the way of wisdom; I have led thee in right paths. When thou goest, thy steps shall not be straitened; and when thou runnest, ***thou shalt not stumble.*** Take fast hold of instruction; let her not go: keep her, for she is thy life" (Prov. 4:11-13).

The balance of the chapter describes ***the city captured*** (vv.6-8), ***the city looted*** (vv.9-10), and ***the city destroyed*** (vv.11-13).

NAHUM

5) The Execution of Judgment on Nineveh (Continued)

Read Chapter 2:6-13

In our previous paper, we began to trace the sequence of events in Chapter 2, and noticed that in verses 1-2, we have the ***city besieged***, and in verses 3-5, the ***city attacked.*** There are three more stages in the prophetic narrative: verses 6-8, the ***city capture***d; verses 9-10, the ***city looted***; verses 11-13, the ***city destroyed.***

This brings us to:

3) THE CITY CAPTURED, vv.6-8

"Wherefore let him that thinketh he standeth take heed lest he fall" (1 Cor. 10:12). Nineveh certainly thought herself absolutely secure. This is clear from two things which are said in these verses:

- "The gates of the rivers shall be opened, and the palace shall be dissolved. And ***Huzzab*** shall be led away captive." The name "Huzzab" means 'fixed' or 'established' and refers, not to a person, but to Nineveh itself. The city, which thought herself immovable and impregnable, is "led away captive". The lesson for us is very clear indeed.

We have already noticed "that the capture of Nineveh was due to divine intervention in the form of an unprecedented flood, which destroyed a large part of the wall, thus giving the enemy access to the city" (Hobart E. Freeman. *Nahum, Zephaniah, Habakkuk. Minor Prophets of the Seventh Century B.C.* p.28). The actual words, "the gates of the rivers shall be opened", have been variously explained, and interested readers are referred to more detailed commentaries.

- "But Nineveh is of old like ***a pool of water***: yet they shall flee away. Stand, stand, shall they cry; but none shall look back." The city seemed invulnerable. It was situated by the river Tigris and surrounded by water. But its inhabitants fled in terror. Proverbs tells us, "Pride goeth before destruction, and an haughty spirit before a fall" (16:18).

Thus far, we have endeavoured to learn some lessons from Nineveh's defeat. But there is something to learn from the victory, bearing in mind that the joint army was a divine instrument to punish Nineveh. Because they were acting, albeit unconsciously, on God's behalf, the greatest possible obstacles were overcome by divine intervention. This recalls the language of Luke 1 verse 37, "For with God nothing shall be impossible".

4) THE CITY LOOTED, vv.9-10

These verses are quite self-explanatory. "Take ye the spoil of silver, take the spoil of gold: for there is none end of the store and glory (wealth) out of all the pleasant furniture" (v.9).

Nineveh acquired its immense wealth by plundering others, so there is, presumably, no direct application to ourselves! But these verses certainly remind us of what Paul called "uncertain riches". The Lord Jesus taught, "Lay not up for yourselves treasures upon earth, where moth and rust doth corrupt, and where thieves break through and steal: but lay up for yourselves treasures in heaven" (Matt. 6:19-21). Paul reminds us that "they that ***will be rich*** ('desire to be rich', JND) fall into temptation and a snare, and into many foolish and hurtful lusts, which drown men in destruction and perdition. For the love of money is the root of all evil" (1 Tim. 6:9-10). He continues, "Charge them that ***are rich*** in this world, that they be not highminded, nor trust in uncertain riches" (1 Tim. 6:17). Some people desire to be rich, and some are rich. The assembly at Smyrna was in poverty materially, but rich spiritually (Rev. 2:9): the assembly at Laodicea was rich materially, but poor spiritually (Rev. 3:17).

Where does ***our*** prosperity lie? Material prosperity is subject to falling interest rates, Stock Market crashes, larceny, and all the rest of the hazards. We must remember the parable of the rich fool (Luke 12:16-20). It illustrated the Saviour's words, "Take heed, and beware of covetousness: for a man's life consisteth not in the abundance of the things which he possesseth" (v.15), and the parable is followed by the words, "So is he that layeth up treasure for himself, and is not rich toward God" (v.21).

While we may not be enjoying material prosperity, we should certainly be enjoying, like Gaius, 'prosperity of ***soul***'. See 3 John 2.

5) THE CITY DESTROYED, vv.11-13

"Be not deceived; God is not mocked: for whatsoever a man soweth, that shall he also reap" (Gal. 6:7). Nineveh reaped what she sowed. She had acted like a ravenous lion. Her cruelty and violence were unparalleled. "The image of the lion, which the prophet uses to depict Assyria, is appropriate, because sculptured lions were frequently stationed at the gates of temples and palaces to act as guardians, and because of the lion's cruel, ravenous nature. Nineveh, moreover, was filled with the spoil of many nations, as a lion's den is of its prey" (Hobart E. Freeman).

God said through Habakkuk, "Woe to him that buildeth a town with blood, and stablisheth a city by iniquity!" (Hab. 2:12). While the Median-Babylonian - Scythian alliance was responsible for destroying this den of lions, the initiative for doing so belonged to God Himself. "Behold, ***I am against thee***, saith the LORD of hosts, and ***I will*** burn her chariots in the smoke ... and ***I will*** cut off thy prey from the earth" (v.13). The nation that specialised in violent conquest was conquered violently. The words, "the voice of thy messengers shall no more be heard", mean, amongst other things, that the voices of Tartan, Rabsaris and Rab-shakeh (2 Kings 18:17) were silenced for ever.

We too have to contend with a lion. Peter wrote: "Be sober, be vigilant; because your adversary the devil, as a roaring lion, walketh about, seeking whom he may devour" (1 Pet. 5:8). But we are encouraged by John: "Greater is he that is in you, than he that is in the world" (1 John 4:4).

Chapter 1 ends with messengers bearing good tidings: "Behold upon the mountains the feet of him that bringeth good tidings, that publisheth peace" (v.15). Chapter 2 ends with messengers made redundant! Once they carried news of Assyrian victories, and demands for tribute from conquered peoples. But not any more: "The voice of thy messengers shall no more be heard".

We must conclude by noting that there is a better way to sow, and a better way to reap (cf. Gal. 6:7): "Let us not be weary in well doing: for in due season we shall reap, if we faint not" (Gal. 6:9).

NAHUM

6) The Explanation of Judgment on Nineveh

Read Chapter 3:1-4

Nahum 1 ***announces*** the destruction of Nineveh, Nahum 2 ***describes*** the destruction of Nineveh and Nahum 3 ***explains*** the judgment of Nineveh. We have already heard God say, "I will make thy grave, for thou art vile" (1:14). We shall now see that this statement was fully justified. Nineveh was certainly "vile", and thoroughly merited divine judgment.

In this connection we should notice -

1) THE CRUELTY OF NINEVEH, vv.1-3

"Woe to the bloody city! it is all full of lies and robbery; the prey departeth not" (v.1). The violence of Nineveh is well documented. 'The Assyrians were noted for their ruthlessness and shameful atrocities against other nations. Their victims were mutilated, beheaded, or burned to death. Captured leaders were often flayed and had their skins spread upon the walls of the city. The Assyrian kings boasted of their calculated cruelty in order to instil terror in their enemies. They cut off limbs or blinded them, while others were impaled on stakes or dragged to death behind chariots' (Hobart E. Freeman. *Nahum, Zephaniah, Habakkuk. Minor Prophets of the Seventh Century B.C.* p.35).

The same writer quotes several inscriptions recovered from Assyrians ruins. Here are two of them:

- ***Shalmaneser 111***: 'I stormed and captured the city. Multitudes of his warriors I slew. His spoil I carried off. A pyramid of heads I reared in front of his city. Their youths and their maidens I burnt up in the flames.'

- ***Ashurbanipal*** describes his treatment of a captured leader as follows: 'I pierced his chin with my keen hand dagger. Through his jaw I passed a rope, put a dog chain upon him and made him occupy a kennel of the east gate of Nineveh.'

It's nightmarish, isn't it? Verses 2-3 describe a typical Assyrian attack, with great "multitude of slain, and a great number of carcases". No wonder God says, "Woe to the ***bloody*** city!" Then there were the "lies and robbery", which imply treachery and deceit. All this reminds us, "Righteousness exalteth a nation: but sin is a reproach to any people" (Prov. 14:34). We have already noted the words of Habakkuk 2 verse 12, "Woe to him that buildeth a town with blood, and stablisheth a city by iniquity".

If we feel tempted to regard all this as past history, perhaps we ought to think again. We may not be guilty of physical violence, but there are other types of violence. Hence Paul writes, "Use not liberty for an occasion to the flesh, but by love serve one another. For all the law is fulfilled in one word, even in this; Thou shalt love thy neighbour as thyself. ***But if ye bite and devour one another, take heed that ye be not consumed one of another"*** (Gal. 5:13-15). James talks about "wars and fightings among you" (James 4:1). The violence of Nineveh was one contributory factor to its disappearance without trace for hundreds of years, and assemblies have also disappeared because of failure to put away "bitterness, and wrath, and anger, and clamour, and evil speaking" (Eph. 4:31).

2) THE SUBTILTY OF NINEVEH, v.4

Here is a second reason for divine judgment: "Because of the multitude of the whoredoms of the wellfavoured harlot". The word, "wellfavoured", refers to the attractiveness and seductiveness of Nineveh. There was another side to Assyrian depravity. We have noted her power to enslave by violence, but that was not the only way in which she dominated others. See Ezekiel 23 verses 5-7: "And Aholah (Samaria) played the harlot when she was mine; and she doted on her lovers, ***on the Assyrians*** her neighbours, which were clothed with blue, captains and rulers, all of them desirable young men, horsemen riding upon horses. Thus she committed her whoredoms with them, with all them that were the chosen ***men of Assyria***, and with all on whom she doted; ***with all their idols she defiled herself***". King Ahaz certainly treated Assyria as a "wellfavoured harlot" (see 2 Kings 16:7-9). He effectively made Judah a constituent part of the Assyrian Empire to the extent that his son, Hezekiah, was charged with rebellion by Sennacherib (See 2 Kings 18:20). Assyria brought nations under her power by making them depend on her, for which, of course, she extracted her price. It is interesting to notice the tactics employed against Hezekiah. The Assyrians ultimately resorted to outright threats, but before doing so, they made an attractive proposition. Read all about it in 2 Kings 18 verses 31-32. The Assyrians could charm as well as threaten.

James points out the lesson for ourselves. With characteristic forthrightness, he warns: “Ye adulterers and adulteresses, know ye not that the friendship of the world is enmity with God? Whosoever therefore ***will be*** a friend of the world is the enemy of God” (James 4:4) We must be careful not to let the world allure us in the way that Nineveh allured the nations. Notice what Hosea says about all this: “Ephraim also is like a silly dove without heart: they call to Egypt, they go to ***Assyria***” (Hosea 7:11). With this result: “Ephraim shall return to Egypt, and they shall eat unclean things in ***Assyria***” (Hosea 9:3). The lesson is clear: Court the favour of the world, and it will make a takeover bid for you.

3) THE SORCERY OF NINEVEH, v.4

Nineveh is described as “***the mistress of witchcrafts***”, as well as “the wellfavoured harlot”. Paul comments on the relationship between the two as follows: “What say I then? that the idol is any thing, or that which is offered in sacrifice to idols is any thing? But I say, that the things which the Gentiles sacrifice, they sacrifice to devils, and not to God” (1 Cor. 10:19-20). Idol temples were demon temples.

Nineveh was succeeded by Babylon, and Isaiah refers to her “enchantments ... sorceries ... astrologers ... stargazers” and “monthly prognosticators” (Isaiah 47:9-13). They would all prove useless. The New Testament anticipates an increase in occult practices and power in the last days. See 1 Timothy 4 verse 1, “Now the Spirit speaketh expressly, that in the latter times some shall depart from the faith, giving heed to seducing spirits, and doctrines of devils”. The Scriptures expressly prohibit all involvement in the ‘black arts’. In this connection it is well-worth noting Deuteronomy 18 verses 9-12. Do notice the meaning of the terms employed: “Thou shalt not learn to do after the abominations of those nations. There shall not be found among you any one that maketh his son or his daughter to pass through the fire, or that useth divinations ***(fortune telling),*** or an observer of times

(astrology), or an enchanter ***(magician)***, or a witch ***(sorcerer)***, or a charmer ***(hypnotist)***, or a consulter with familiar spirits ***(medium possessed with a spirit "guide")***, or a wizard ***(clairvoyant)***, or a necromancer ***(medium who consults the dead)***. For all that do these things are an abomination unto the LORD".

The balance of the chapter describes the judgment which Nineveh so clearly deserved.

NAHUM

7) The Explanation of Judgment on Nineveh (Continued)

Read Chapter 3:5-19

The opening section of Chapter 3 sets out the reasons for the destruction of Nineveh. The passage refers to her cruelty, subtility and sorcery (vv.1-4). The remaining verses of the chapter describe the judgment so richly deserved by Nineveh.

1) NINEVEH WOULD BE PUBLICLY DISGRACED, vv.5-7

This is the force of verses 5-6: "Behold, I am against thee, saith the LORD of hosts; and I will discover thy skirts upon thy face, and I will show the nations thy nakedness, and the kingdoms thy shame. And I will cast abominable filth upon thee, and make thee vile, and will set thee as a gazingstock".

In reading these words, we must remember that Nineveh has just been described as "the wellfavoured harlot" and would be treated accordingly. The downfall of Babylon is similarly described in Isaiah 47 verses 1-3. The nation which had so openly enslaved others by cruelty and subtilty would be openly humiliated. History furnishes us with more examples, and all underline the New Testament statement: "Be not deceived; God is not mocked: for whatsoever a man soweth, that shall he also reap" (Gal. 6:7). The law of sowing and reaping is all-embracing. Society is reaping the harvest of indiscipline in family, school, and social life. The lie of evolution has destroyed the sense of accountability to God, with the result that "there is no fear of God before their eyes" (Rom. 3:18). The "wise and prudent" evolutionist can sneer as much as he likes at the simple faith of the "babe", but it is the "babe" that enjoys the truth imparted by the "Lord of heaven and earth" (Matt. 11:25).

There would be no help for Nineveh when disaster struck the city. She would be friendless and alone. "And it shall come to pass, that all they that look upon thee shall flee from thee, and say, Nineveh is laid waste: who will bemoan her? Whence shall I seek comforters (there would be no Nahums) for thee?" (v.7). This is hardly surprising when we remember the way in which Nahum had treated other people. The Lord Jesus taught, "With what measure ye mete, it shall be measured to you again" (Matt. 7:2).

We are told, amongst other things, that Nineveh would become a "gazingstock". If you would like to fulfil this yourself, see the Addendum.

2) NINEVEH HAD FAILED TO LEARN FROM HISTORY, vv.8-10

"Art thou better than populous No, that was situate among the rivers ... ?" This refers to the city of No-amon in Upper Egypt. It is better known as Thebes, which was the name given to it by the Greeks. Its ruins survive at Karnak and Luxor. The city was said to have a hundred gates. It was situated on the Nile and protected by canals. The Nile is here called "the sea" which, of course, refers to the result of the annual flooding. It resembled a sea when this happened. The references in verse 9 are interesting. "Ethiopia" is self-explanatory. "Put" refers to Somalia, and "Lubim" to Libya. The Egyptian kings ruled a mighty empire as implied in the words, "it was infinite", but Thebes was captured in 663 B.C. by none other than the Assyrians under Ashurbanipal, and they displayed their customary cruelty. (See v.10.) The strength and allies of Thebes did not save her: "Yet was she carried away, she went into captivity".

"Populous No" thought herself invincible, but the Assyrians proved otherwise (v.10). But, now, the seemingly invincible Assyrian capital was about to fall (vv.11-12). This teaches us at least two important lessons.

- ***We cannot afford to ignore past warnings.*** God makes this clear through Zephaniah: "I have cut off the nations: their towers are desolate; I made their streets waste, that none passeth by: their cities are destroyed, so that there is no man, that there is none inhabitant. I said, ***Surely thou wilt fear me, thou wilt receive instruction:*** so their dwelling should not be cut off, howsoever I punished them: but they arose early, and corrupted all their doings" (Zeph. 3:6-7).

- ***We must never think that we are beyond defeat.*** Thebes was not preserved by its "rampart" and "wall" when the Assyrians attacked, and the "infinite" strength of its empire was insufficient when the battle raged. We could write over "Populous No" the following words, "Let him that thinketh he standeth take heed lest he fall" (1 Cor. 10:12). Paul was obliged to write to the assembly at Thessalonica, with all its excellent qualities, "I sent to know your faith, ***lest by some means the tempter have tempted you***, and our labour be in vain" (1 Thess. 3:5). Who would have thought that the Lord Jesus should have to say, "I have somewhat against thee", to the assembly at Ephesus? Ephesus, with all its illustrious spiritual history! But what about ourselves?

3) NINEVEH WOULD BE COMPREHENSIVELY DESTROYED, vv.11-19

God now describes the coming destruction of Nineveh in various ways: it would be all-embracing.

a) "Thy strong holds", v.12

"All thy strong holds shall be like fig trees with the firstripe figs; if they be shaken, they shall even fall into the mouth of the eater." That's how easily it would happen! See verse 14, "Fortify thy strong holds". This refers to the work required to keep the city repaired and intact. It takes little imagination to see the defenders feverishly making bricks. But all to no avail: "There shall the fire devour thee; the sword shall cut thee off, it shall eat thee up like the cankerworm (the licking locust)" (v.15). "Because of man's powerlessness to stop them, the locust plague is used in Scripture to symbolize the absolute destruction wrought by enemy forces" (Hobart E. Freeman). (See also Joel 1:4; 2:1-11.) The defenders may be as "many as the cankerworm" and as "many as the locusts" (v.15), but that wouldn't help either. It's worth saying at this juncture that we must not think for one moment that a large assembly is necessarily a strong assembly.

b) "Thy people", v.13

"Behold, thy people in the midst of thee are women." There are similar references elsewhere in the Old Testament. (See Isaiah 19:16, Jeremiah 50:37; 51:30.) It's hardly necessary to say that these references are not intended to discredit the 'fair sex'. They simply state that "Nineveh's defenders ... would be unable to demonstrate manly valour to fight for the city" (*Unger's Commentary on the Old Testament* p.1892). We are urged,

"Quit you like men, be strong" (1 Cor. 16:13). Are we "Strong in the Lord, and in the power of his might"? (Eph. 6:10).

c) "Thy merchants", v.16

"Thou hast multiplied thy merchants above the stars of heaven." Political power requires economic power. See Revelation 17-18. The commercial strength of Nineveh was doomed. "The cankerworm spreadeth himself out and flieth away" (JND). The invaders would strip the city of its riches and leave with the spoil. See our comments on Chapter 2 verse 9, and remember the words of the Lord Jesus: "What shall it profit a man, if he shall gain the whole world, and lose his own soul?" (Mark 8:36).

d) "Thy crowned ... thy captains", v.17

"Thy crowned are as the locusts, and thy captains as the great grasshoppers, which camp in the hedges in the cold day, but when the sun ariseth they flee away." Cold weather deprives the locust of its powers of flight, but this returns with the warmth of the sun. They fly with a change in climate, just like some Christians! Paul had to say, "Demas hath forsaken me, having loved this present world". But he also said, "Luke is with me" (2 Tim. 4:10-11). We should read on in the same chapter, at least until verses 16-17, and then ask ourselves how ***we*** would react when the pressure is mounting, and difficulties loom ahead.

e) "Thy shepherds ... thy nobles", v.18

"Thy shepherds slumber, O king of Assyria: thy nobles shall dwell in the dust." In other words, they will die. As a result, "Thy people is scattered upon the mountains, and no man gathereth them". Compare 1 Kings 22 verse 17, "And he (Micaiah) said, I saw all Israel scattered upon the hills, as sheep that have not a shepherd: and the LORD said, These have no master". Ahab was to die, and his people would be scattered. Another Shepherd was smitten, but He rose from the dead, and gathered the scattered sheep. See Matthew 26 verse 31, which cites Zechariah 13 verse 7.

God has shepherds too. See, for example, 1 Peter 5 verses 1-4. When there's something wrong with spiritual shepherds, it's not long before the flock is scattered. Sometimes they are given to spiritual "slumber". ***A New Testament shepherd must be constantly awake, and constantly diligent.***

He is certainly not responsible ***to*** the flock, but he is certainly responsible ***for*** the flock. He is "the steward of God" (Titus 1:7).

f) "Thy bruise ... thy wound", v.19

"There is no healing of thy bruise; thy wound is grievous; all that hear the bruit (report) of thee shall clap the hands over thee: for upon whom hath not thy wickedness passed continually?" The word "bruise" comes from a root meaning, 'to break or tear in pieces'. When the blow comes, it will be fatal. The closing question - "For upon whom hath not thy wickedness passed continually?" - stresses the duration of Assyria's wickedness, and at the same time, the duration of God's forbearance. But now judgment comes. The city of Nineveh had repented at the preaching of Jonah, but time had proved this repentance to be shallow. The city, capital of Assyria, returned to its former cruelty and oppression. God does not now "turn and repent, and turn away from his fierce anger" (Jonah 3:9-10). The book of Jonah demonstrates the "goodness" of God: the book of Nahum demonstrates the "severity of God" (Rom. 11:22). Hobart E. Freeman puts it as follows: "In the judicial punishment of Nineveh is seen the unchanging truth that ***righteousness will ultimately triumph, for kingdoms built upon wickedness and tyranny must fall***".

ADDENDUM

"I ... will set thee as a gazingstock"

Next time you are in London, take time (if you can) to visit the Department of Assyriology in the British Museum. Once *in situ*, just stand there and gaze! Behold the results of Professor Layard's excavations at Nineveh! Bible prophecy is always 'spot on' – down to the minutest detail!

HABAKKUK

by
John M Riddle

HABAKKUK

1) INTRODUCTION

We call Habakkuk and his colleagues 'The Minor Prophets', but this is neither accurate nor complimentary! On the contrary, they were 'Major Men of God'! Their books are only 'minor' in terms of size when compared with those of Isaiah, Jeremiah and Ezekiel. These comparatively small books have been beautifully described as 'the twelve-jewelled crown of the Old Testament'. Taken together, they have been called 'The Book of the Twelve'.

Jeremiah tells us that the true prophet "stood in the counsel of the LORD, and hath perceived and heard his word" (Jer. 23:18). He also tells us, on eleven occasions, that God rose up early to speak to Israel through the prophets. (See, for example, Jeremiah 7: 25.) Habakkuk was one of them, and it might be helpful to see his position in relation to the other 'writing prophets'. So:

1) THE POSITION

Habakkuk belonged to the Seventh Century, i.e. 700-601 B.C. It would be interesting to commence at the exodus from Egypt and construct a complete table of the prophets sent by God. It would begin with Moses (Deut. 18:15; 34:10) and Aaron (Exodus 7:1), and include a great number of men (and some women), some named and some unnamed. The 'writing prophets' alone cover five centuries, viz:

Fifth/Sixth Century prophets: Haggai/ Zechariah/ Malachi/ Ezekiel/ Daniel.
Seventh Century prophets: Nahum/ **Habakkuk**/ Zephaniah/ Obadiah/ Jeremiah.
Eighth Century prophets: Hosea/ Amos/ Micah/ Isaiah.
Ninth Century prophets: Jonah and possibly Joel.

Since Obadiah evidently prophesied after the fall of Jerusalem (see verses

10-14), he probably should be transferred to the beginning of the Sixth Century. In any case, the above table is rather ‘rough and ready’ in the extreme, but it could easily be ‘fine-tuned’ to produce a more accurate picture. The Ninth Century (900-801 B.C.) brings us to the era of Elijah and Elisha, which reminds us that there were a vast number of ‘non-writing prophets’. These could be incorporated in a more comprehensive table. For example, the Tenth Century introduces us to the unnamed prophet who cried against Jeroboam’s altar and the “old prophet in Bethel” (1 Kings 13).

This proves that God was not exaggerating when He said, “Since the day that your fathers came forth out of the land of Egypt unto this day I have even sent unto you all my servants the prophets, ***daily*** rising up early and sending them” (Jer. 7:25). He was never silent. Whilst the oft-quoted words in Acts 14 verse 17 do not refer to the prophets, we can ***apply*** them in that way, and say that God “left not himself without witness” so far as the prophetic testimony was concerned. This should encourage us today: through His servants, and sometimes without them, there will be an ongoing testimony to “all the counsel of God” (Acts 20:27), and even when Jerusalem becomes the darkest moral blot on earth, He will give power to His “two witnesses ... these two prophets” (Rev. 11:3-12).

Referring now to the Seventh Century prophets, we should notice the following in connection with Nahum, Habakkuk and Zephaniah:

Nahum. The prophet refers to the destruction of Thebes (called ‘No’, Nahum 3:8: margin ‘No-Amon’) and coming destruction of Nineveh. These events took place in 663 B.C. and 612 B.C. respectively.

Habakkuk. He prophesied between the destruction of Nineveh and the invasion of Judaea by the Babylonians, i.e. between 612 and 605 B.C. The violence and lawlessness of Judah prior to the Babylonian captivity points to the end of the southern kingdom. The prophecy probably belongs to the reign of Jehoiakim, Josiah’s second son.

Zephaniah. He preached “in the days of Josiah”, Chapter 1 verse 1. Before the destruction of Nineveh (Chapter 2:13) in 612 B.C., and evidently before Josiah’s great reforms in 621 B.C.

2) THE PROPHET

We know little about him, but he was evidently a man with a deep concern for God's people. He was a man of prayer: he prayed consistently: see Chapter 1 verse 2. He was a man of faith: he expected God to answer: see Chapter 2 verse 1. He was a man with a concern for God's glory: he recognised His greatness: see Chapter 2 verse 12. He was a man of praise: see Chapter 3.

His name means 'embracing' or 'enfolding'. In the words of J. B. Hewitt: "The book is built up around the meaning of his name. He 'embraced' his God in ***prayer***, for he was perplexed. See Chapter 1 verse 4 and verses 12-15. He 'embraced' God by ***faith***, for he expected a solution to his problems. See Chapter 2 verses 1-4, 14, 20. He 'embraced' God with ***songs of victory,*** as he anticipated the glorious triumph of God over all evil. See Chapter 3 verses 1-19". We can add that he certainly 'embraced' a problem as well! His name could, however, mean 'wrestling' as well as 'embracing'. Perhaps we could say that he 'wrestled' in Chapter 1 and 'embraced' in Chapter 3.

3) THE PROBLEM

Habakkuk had a familiar problem. Why does God tolerate evil? How can He be consistent with Himself and yet permit evil whilst remaining silent? So he begins, "O LORD, how long shall I cry, and thou wilt not hear! Even cry out unto thee of violence, and thou wilt not save!" (Chapter 1:2), and continues, "Wherefore lookest thou upon them that deal treacherously, and holdest thy tongue when the wicked devoureth the man that is more righteous than he?" (Chapter 1:13). Compare Psalm 73: "I was envious at the foolish, when I saw the prosperity of the wicked ... Behold, these are the ungodly, who prosper in the world; they increase in riches ... When I thought to know this, it was too painful for me; ***until*** I went into the sanctuary of God" (vv.3, 12, 16-17).

4) THE PATTERN

Habakkuk is a unique book. It is essentially a dialogue between God and Habakkuk, and we are eavesdroppers! The nation is not directly addressed by the prophet. The book may be divided into five sections. Habakkuk speaks three times, and God speaks twice:

i) ***Habakkuk's Problem, 1:1-4.*** Why are the wicked unjudged? It is the cry of a righteous man surrounded by wickedness. He had prayed for a long time, but the situation was worsening. God seemed inactive.

ii) ***God's Answer, 1:5-11.*** He ***is*** doing something about the situation: the Chaldeans were coming as His instrument of punishment.

iii) ***Habakkuk's Protest, 1:12 - 2:1.*** But the Chaldeans are more wicked than Judah! The prophet questions the moral correctness of God's answer.

iv) ***God's Answer, 2:2-20.*** "Wait for it" (2:3). He will deal with the Chaldeans (verses 5-13). But beyond that, He has a grand objective: "The earth will be filled with the knowledge of the glory of the LORD" (v.14). In the meanwhile, "the just shall live by his faith" (v.4).

v) ***Habakkuk's Prayer, 3:1-19.*** The prophecy terminates with sublime faith. "I will rejoice in the LORD, I will joy in the God of my salvation." See verses 17-18.

The nation is not directly addressed by the prophet, as usually happens. We could summarise it as follows: ***Sighing*** (Chapter 1), "Why?"; ***Seeing*** (Chapter 2), "Wait!"; ***Singing*** (Chapter 3), Worship. Or, Habakkuk ***questioning*** Jehovah (Chapter 1); Habakkuk ***waiting*** on Jehovah (Chapter 2); Habakkuk ***rejoicing*** in Jehovah (Chapter 3).

5) THE PURPOSE

The purpose of the book is to strengthen faith. It commences with bewilderment and uncertainty and ends with the prophet treading his "high places" with sure feet. The book has a magnificent conclusion: "Although the fig tree shall not blossom, neither shall fruit be in the vines; the labour of the olive shall fail, and the fields shall yield no meat; the flock shall be cut off from the fold, and there shall be no herd in the stalls: yet I will rejoice in the LORD, I will joy in the God of my salvation" (Chapter 3:17-18). Over the book we could write: "And this is the victory that overcometh the world, even our ***faith***" (1 John 5:4).

The book is cited five times in the New Testament. ***Chapter 2 verse 4*** is quoted in Romans 1 verse 17, Galatians 3 verse 11, and Hebrews 10 verse 38. ***Chapter 1 verse 5*** is quoted in Acts 13 verse 41. ***Chapter 2 verse 3*** is quoted in Hebrews 10 verse 37.

HABAKKUK

2) Chapter 1

As we have already noticed in our introduction, the book of Habakkuk can be divided into five sections: Habakkuk speaks three times and God speaks twice. The book opens with:

1) HABAKKUK'S PROBLEM, vv.1-4

"The burden which Habakkuk the prophet did see. O LORD, how long shall I cry, and thou wilt not hear! even cry out unto thee of violence, and thou wilt not save!" (vv.1-2). We should notice at least two things in these introductory verses: ***(a)*** his calling (v.1), and ***(b)*** his concern (vv.2-4).

a) His calling, v.1

"The burden which Habakkuk ***the prophet*** did see." See also Chapter 3 verse 1, "A prayer of Habakkuk ***the prophet*** upon Shigionoth". He firmly recognised his calling from God.

Like Habakkuk, we must recognise ***our*** calling from God and actively pursue it. "Having then gifts differing according to the grace that is given to us, whether prophecy, let us prophesy according to the proportion of faith; or ministry, let us wait on our ministering: or he that teacheth, on teaching; or he that exhorteth, on exhortation" (Rom. 12:6-8). The prophet recognised two things:

- He had ***received*** a vision from God: "The burden which Habakkuk the prophet did ***see***". (Compare Isaiah 1:1.) So the word of God was revealed to him. He was unlike the false prophets who "speak a vision of their own heart, and not out of the mouth of the LORD" (Jer. 23:16). This reminds us that "if any man speak, let him speak as the oracles of God" (1 Pet. 4:11).

- He ***felt*** the weight of the word of God. "The ***burden*** which Habakkuk the prophet did see." The word, "burden" (Hebrew, *'massa'),* means a heavy or weighty thing, and is used in the Old Testament to describe a heavy or weighty message or oracle. Compare, for example, Malachi 1 verse 1, "The burden of the word of the LORD to Israel by Malachi". (See also, for example, Isaiah 13:1, 15:1; 17:1; Nahum 1:1. Read Jeremiah 23:31-40.) The message was weighty in itself, and its weight was felt by the servant. Habakkuk was unlike the false prophets described by Zephaniah as "light and treacherous persons" (Zeph. 3:4).

So the prophet related what he saw (hence the word "seer": see, for example, 1 Samuel 9:9), and what he saw was a burden to him. This raises two questions for us: firstly, are ***we*** conveying the word of God without addition or amendment? and, secondly, do ***we*** feel the weight of the word of God? We can never expect to convey it effectively to others unless we feel its weight and value ourselves.

b) His concern, vv.2-4

Habakkuk's description of civil disobedience leads us to the conclusion that he preached during the reign of Jehoiakim (see, for example, Jeremiah 22:1) rather than in the reign of godly Josiah. Habakkuk's problem centred on three things:

i) Unanswered prayer, v.2. Habakkuk took far more than a casual interest in his circumstances. He felt the situation acutely. "O LORD, how long shall I ***cry*** *(shava*, to cry aloud), and thou wilt not hear! even ***cry*** (*zaaq,* to cry out) out unto thee of violence, and thou wilt not save!" Habakkuk did not go to the ***people*** with ***preaching:*** he went to ***God*** in ***prayer.*** He kept on grappling with the problem.

The believer who goes through life without asking questions must live on another planet! Habakkuk was perplexed by what he saw. Why did God allow such conduct? There was no answer to his prayers. We can sympathise with Habakkuk. We all have this difficulty at times! Problems are inevitable when we approach God with fixed ideas and prescribed answers! ***We*** think we know how God ought to work! As we shall see, God answered Habakkuk's prayers in a most unexpected way! He answered his prayers by allowing things to become even worse, before they became better. At the end of it all the man who prayed gave himself to praise!

All this reminds us that we ***can*** trust in the Lord. We must also remember that in some circumstances, He may say 'No', and that this is as much an answer as any other! We must also remember, "If I regard iniquity in my heart, the Lord will not hear me" (Psalm 66:18). It has been said that 'there is no such thing as unanswered prayer, but there is such a thing as unheard prayer'. In this connection, we must notice:

ii) Unanswered questions, v.2. "O LORD, ***how long*** shall I cry, and thou wilt not hear ... ***Why*** dost thou shew me iniquity, and cause me to behold grievance?" We often feel like Isaiah when he said, "Verily thou art a God that hideth thyself" (Isaiah 45:15). Matthew Henry observes: "He may hide Himself, but He does not absent Himself!" As D. M. Lloyd-Jones observes, "If God were unkind enough to answer some of our prayers at once, we should be very impoverished Christians".

iii) Unrestrained evil, vv.3-4. As we have seen, the prophet felt the situation deeply: ***"I cry"*** (v.2). Evil was not restrained (v.3), and law was not exercised (v.4). Those entrusted with the law did not implement it properly and justly. Righteousness and judgment were not exercised and, even worse, wrong judgment proceeded. Habakkuk uses a chilling vocabulary: "grievance (vexation) … spoiling (devastation) … violence … strife … contention". He was concerned for righteousness. The righteous were in the minority, and therefore proper judgment was not upheld. We are all too familiar with the situation. This is precisely the position in our own land.

We can hear the despondent notes in Habakkuk's voice. Just listen to his perplexity - "Why dost thou ...?"; to his weariness - "How long?"; to his frustration - "Wilt not hear"; to his indignation - "The wicked doth compass about the righteous". Here, then, is Habakkuk's problem.

2) GOD'S ANSWER, vv.5-11

Habakkuk had cried, "How long?" God answers, 'Now!' "I will work a work in ***your days***". We should notice three things here: ***(a)*** the certainty of divine judgment (v.5); ***(b)*** the effect of divine judgment (v.5); ***(c)*** the instrument of divine judgment (vv.6-11).

a) The certainty of divine judgment, v.5

"Behold ye among the heathen, and regard ... For, lo, I raise up the

Chaldeans." Prayer ***had*** been heard: God ***was*** doing something about the situation! It is as if God said, 'Stop, Habakkuk. You have used your voice, now use your eyes!' "Behold ... regard." We can be certain that He will always act. He is longsuffering, but He does act. Compare 2 Peter 3 verses 9-10: "The Lord is not slack concerning his promise, as some men count slackness; but is longsuffering to us-ward, not willing that any should perish, but that all should come to repentance. But the day of the Lord ***will*** come."

This was not quite the answer Habakkuk expected. God was going to use foreigners to correct His people. "Behold ye among the ***heathen***." We might have expected God to intervene in judgment on the judiciary. We might have expected divine intervention by plague, or perhaps the withholding of the dew and rain, as on other occasions (see, for example, 1 Kings 17:1).

We therefore learn ***(i)*** that God achieves His purposes in unexpected ways, and ***(ii)*** that evil, whether in the world or amongst His professing people, will ***not*** remain unpunished. God is not inactive when His word is flouted. We must notice His sovereignty in human history. ***"I*** raise up the Chaldeans" (v.6). The Babylonian invasion was ***not*** a quirk of fate! As we have noticed, Habakkuk would not have to wait too long before it happened: "I will work a work in ***your*** days" (v.5). Divine intervention was imminent.

b) The effect of divine judgment, v.5

It would cause intense wonder and amazement. "I will work a work in your days, which ye will not believe, though it be told you." How would it cause wonder and amazement? Through the Chaldeans, God would bring overwhelming devastation and captivity upon His people. The words, "which ye will not believe", mean, 'God wouldn't do a thing like that! What, use the Chaldeans? Impossible!' People just would not believe the prophet.

This passage is cited in Acts 13 verses 40-41: "Beware therefore, lest that come upon you, which is spoken of in the ***prophets;*** behold, ye despisers, and wonder, and perish: for I work a work in your days, a work which ye shall in no wise believe, though a man declare it unto you". The reason for coming judgment is found in Acts 13 verse 27, "For they that dwell at Jerusalem, and their rulers, because they knew him not, nor yet the voices of the ***prophets*** which are read every sabbath day, they have fulfilled them in condemning him". Through Habakkuk, God announced the overwhelming destruction of His people, and this was exactly what Paul announced in Acts 13. In the

Old Testament, God raised up the Chaldeans to judge His people: in the New Testament, God raised up the Romans.

c) The instrument of divine judgment, vv.6-11

"For, lo, I raise up the Chaldeans." (This refers to the Chaldean period of Babylonian rule.) God is the God of history. "The most High ruleth in the kingdom of men, and giveth it to whomsoever he will" (Dan. 4:25). But He can remove them too! Nothing that occurs in history is outside the divine programme. Things don't just happen! But we should remember that divine judgment on Israel is never an end in itself: it is always related to their future blessing. This was the case in the past. In the days of the Judges, "The anger of the LORD was hot against Israel, and he sold them into the hand of Chushan-rishathaim king of Mesopotamia" (3:8); "The LORD strengthened Eglon the king of Moab against Israel" (3:12); "The LORD delivered them into the hand of Midian seven years" (6:1). In each case, God was intent on the repentance and cleansing of His people from idolatry. This was also His intention in the Assyrian invasion: "O Assyrian, the rod of mine anger, and the staff in their hand is mine indignation ... I will send him against an hypocritical nation, and against the people of my wrath will I give him a charge" (Isaiah 10:5-6). The periods of captivity in the book of Judges, and the Assyrian and Babylonian invasions, were ordered by God for the ultimate benefit of His people. We should note the following in connection with the Chaldeans:

i) Their character, vv.6-7. They are "bitter and hasty ... terrible and dreadful". The words, "their judgment and their dignity shall proceed of themselves", means that they were "a law unto themselves and promote their own honour" (M. C. Unger).

ii) Their conquests, vv.8-10. They are swift ... fierce ... rapacious ... irresistible. "They shall come all for violence." Violence (vv.2-3) would be met with violence (v.9): "They gather captives as the sand" (JND). Note reference to siege mounds: "They shall deride every strong hold; for they shall heap dust, and take it" (v.10).

iii) Their confidence, v.11: "Then shall his mind change, and he shall pass over, and offend (that is, exceed the limit intended by God), imputing this his power unto his god" or 'Then will his mind change, and he will pass on, and become guilty: this his power is become his god' (JND). (The R.V.

reads, "even he whose might is his god".) The Chaldeans would be drunk with success, failing to realise that God had raised them up.

Failure to recognise this brings disaster. In Daniel 2, Nebuchadnezzar was told, "Thou art this head of gold" (v.38). In Chapter 3, he makes a similar image, but completely of gold (v.1). In Chapter 4, he is taught a salutary lesson (vv.31-37). In Chapter 5, another man (Belshazzar) failed to learn the lesson (v.22)!

3) HABAKKUK'S PROTEST, 1:12 - 2:1

While Habakkuk now understood a great deal more than at the beginning, a big problem loomed before him. "Wherefore lookest thou upon them that deal treacherously, and holdest thy tongue when the wicked devoureth the man that is more righteous than he?" The Chaldeans were thoroughly bad, and it just didn't seem right that God should use people like that to chasten His own people. How did this agree with the character of God who is "of purer eyes than to behold evil, and canst not look on iniquity"? (v.13). He understood what God was doing (v.12), but questioned its moral correctness. But, unlike ourselves so often, he didn't try to solve the problem himself: he took it "to the Lord in prayer". In New Testament terms, Habakkuk came "boldly unto the throne of grace" (Heb. 4:16).

There are two ways we can face a problem. Firstly, like Habakkuk: take the problem to God, with faith to believe that He doesn't act contrary to His character. Secondly, like Jonah; don't take the problem to God, and slip away from Him. If we do that we shall certainly pay "the fare thereof" (Jonah 1:3). At first glance, everything seemed to favour Jonah: the ship was there, the captain was favourable, the mariners were helpful, but ...! We must notice the following:

a) His certainty about the nature of God, v.12a

He speaks reverently. Notice how he prefaces his objection. He dwells on the character of God. He finds solid ground for his feet. We need to remember that we see only part of the canvas: God sees the whole picture. Habakkuk rests on what he ***did*** know:

I am not skilled to understand
What God has willed, what God has planned:
I only know at His right hand
Is One who is my Saviour.

Habakkuk knew -

i) That God is eternal. "Art thou not from ***everlasting,*** O LORD my God?" He is outside history, as opposed to the Chaldeans' god - Bel. (See v.11: "imputing this his power unto his god".) There is "nothing more consoling and reassuring when oppressed by the problems of history, and when wondering what is to happen in the world, than to remember that the God whom we worship is outside the flux of history" (D. M. Lloyd-Jones).

ii) That God is faithful. "Art thou not from everlasting, O ***LORD*** my God?" He is 'Jehovah' ("LORD", AV). This is the name that He takes in relation to His people. "I am the LORD ('Jehovah') your God" (Exod. 6:3-7). He was ***still*** the covenant-keeping God. "He hath commanded his covenant for ever" (Psalm 111:9). Therefore, says Habakkuk, "we shall not die" (v.12). That is, be utterly destroyed by the Chaldeans. What a God! The divine name 'Jehovah' enshrines His timelessness and self-existence. Habakkuk knew that God must have the situation under control.

iii) That God is adorable. "Art thou not from everlasting, O LORD my ***God***?" This translates the name *Elohim* which, according to Thomas Newberry, is the plural of *Eloah* from *ahlah,* meaning 'to worship and adore'. 'It presents God as the one supreme object of worship, the Adorable One.'

iv) That God is holy. "Art thou not from everlasting, O LORD my God, mine ***Holy One***?" Habakkuk knew and believed that it was utterly impossible for God to do wrong. He is "of purer eyes than to behold evil, and canst not look on iniquity" (v.13). "Shall not the Judge of all the earth do right?" (Gen. 18:25).

v) That God is immutable. "O LORD (Jehovah), thou hast ordained them for judgment; and, O mighty God (***'O Rock',*** JND), thou hast established them for correction." As 'Jehovah', He is the covenant-keeping God: as the 'Rock', He is steadfast in purpose. The noun "Rock" is a divine title. See, for example, Deuteronomy 32: "I will publish the name of the LORD: ascribe ye greatness unto our God. He is the Rock" (vv.3-4); "But Jeshurun waxed fat, and kicked ... and lightly esteemed the Rock of his salvation" (v.15); "Of the Rock that begat thee thou art unmindful" (v.18); "How should one chase a thousand, and two put ten thousand to flight, except their Rock had sold them" (v.30); "For their rock is not as our Rock" (v.31). When the Lord Jesus said, "Upon this rock, I will build my church", He used language that no Hebrew would ever use of mere man. See also 1 Corinthians 10 verse 4, "They drank of that spiritual Rock that followed them: and that Rock was Christ".

vi) That God is personal. Yes, with all these attributes! "Art thou not from everlasting, O LORD ***my*** God, ***mine*** Holy One?" How wonderful!

We must not forget that in His love for us, God has no desire to harm us. But at the same time, He is sovereign, and too great to be swayed by our prescriptions.

b) His conclusions about the purpose of God, v.12b

"Thou hast ordained them ('him', JND) for judgment ... Thou hast established them ('him', JND) for correction." So Habakkuk understood the role of the Chaldeans. God had raised up the Chaldeans as the instrument by which He would accomplish His purposes for Israel. Notice, again, the absolute sovereignty of God in human affairs. ***"Thou*** hast ordained them for judgment ... ***Thou*** hast established them for correction." Not to destroy them or eliminate them ("We shall not die"), but for their ultimate benefit. Compare Hebrews 12 verses 4-11.

c) His confusion about the ways of God, 1:13 - 2:1

But having stated what he knew about God, Habakkuk now states his problem. We must notice three things here:

i) He addresses the problem to God, vv.13-17

What was the problem? See verse 13: How can God, who hates sin, actually use wicked people to accomplish His aims, without even remonstrating with them? So, in view of known facts about God, Habakkuk asks, "Thou art of purer eyes than to behold evil, and canst not look on iniquity: ***wherefore*** lookest thou upon them that deal treacherously, and holdest thy tongue when the wicked devoureth the man that is more righteous than he?"

In verses 13-15, he tells God about the ***iniquity*** of the Chaldeans, and in verses 16-17, he tells God about the ***idolatry*** of the Chaldeans. The Chaldean is described as a fisherman. (Note J. N. Darby's rendering of verse 14: "And ***thou*** makest men as the fishes of the sea".) "They take up all of them with the angle, they catch them in their net, and gather them in their drag." What escapes the hook, gets caught in the net, and what escapes the trawl net, gets caught in the drag-net. We should notice the following:

- The Chaldeans sacrifice to their net: "Therefore they sacrifice unto their net" (v.16). See Chapter 1 verse 11, 'His power is become his god' (RV).

- The Chaldeans live off their victims: "By them their portion is fat, and their meat plenteous" (v.16).

- The Chaldeans seem set for unending conquest: "Shall they therefore empty their net, and not spare continually to slay the nations?" (v.17). This is not unknown in modern times. We have only to think, for example, of 'ethnic cleansing', and refugees herded from place to place. Like Habakkuk, how can we make sense of it all?

So Habakkuk asks God about it. We must note his frankness here. He tells God exactly what is in his heart. There is nothing wrong in asking, 'Why?', when we do not understand. We must notice, however, that Habakkuk does not speak to God with bitterness and resentment. He is convinced of God's sovereignty and unfailing faithfulness. But as he doesn't understand what is happening, he would like an explanation. Jeremiah was similar: "Righteous art thou, O LORD, when I plead with thee: yet let me talk with thee of thy judgments: Wherefore doth the way of the wicked prosper?" (Jer. 12:1).

ii) He waits for an answer from God, 2:1

He expects an answer, and takes the position of a watchman. He looks away from the problem, and looks to God. Hence the New Testament injunction: "Continue (persevere) in prayer, and watch in the same with thanksgiving" (Col. 4:2).

iii) He expects to be reproved by God, 2:1

"I will stand upon my watch, and set me upon the tower, and will watch to see what he will say unto me, and what I shall answer when I am reproved."

Habakkuk knew that he was wrong, but he wanted to find out ***where*** he was wrong! He expected to be shown his mistake, and to have his arguments corrected.

We now wait for God's answer.

HABAKKUK

(3) *Chapter 2:2-20*

As we have noticed, the prophecy of Habakkuk, which is a dialogue between the prophet and God, can be divided into five sections:

1) Habakkuk's problem, 1:1-4
2) God's answer, 1:5-11
3) Habakkuk's protest, 1:12 - 2:1
4) God's answer, 2:2-20
5) Habakkuk's praise, 3:1-19

In our last study, we left the prophet waiting and watching. "I will stand upon my watch, and set me upon the tower, and will watch to see what he will say unto me, and what I shall answer when I am reproved" (2:1). Habakkuk expected an answer to the problem. He knew that he was wrong, but wanted to know ***where*** he was wrong. He had prayed about the matter, and now he looks expectantly for an explanation and some correction. Notice his words: "I will ***stand***". He was alert and expectant. He ***expected*** an answer. Do ***we*** expect an answer to our prayers? "I will stand upon my watch (watchtower)." He disentangled himself from the noise and clamour of life. Amongst confusion and lawlessness, he goes to his tower. It is there, as we shall see, that he gets things in perspective. Compare Psalm 73 verses 16-17, "When I thought to know this, it was too painful for me; until I went into the sanctuary of God: ***then*** understood I their end". In New Testament terms, this is the ministry of the "closet" (Matt. 6:6). Alone with God. Could God accommodate the man with problems and perplexity? The answer is - 'Yes!' This brings us to:

4) GOD'S ANSWER, 2:2-20

"And the LORD ***answered*** me." There is no censure or reproof. Habakkuk had approached God with genuine concern and openness of heart. We can divide the answer as follows: ***(a)*** the clarity of the answer (v.2); ***(b)*** the certainty of the answer (v.3); ***(c)*** the content of the answer (vv.4-20).

a) The clarity of the answer, v.2

"And the LORD answered me, and said, Write the vision, and make it plain upon tables, that he may run that readeth it." This reminds us of Willam Cowper's hymn:

Blind unbelief is sure to err,
And scan His work in vain;
God is His own interpreter,
And He will make it plain.

i) "Write the vision." (The word "write" occurs sixteen times in Revelation.) This reminds us that "no prophecy of the scripture is of any private interpretation", (2 Pet. 1:20). The prophets did not write down ***their*** interpretation of what they saw: they wrote down ***what*** they saw! We will not have to wait long to discover what Habakkuk actually saw! It is important to notice that he was given the vision while standing on the watchtower. He could only see God's purposes from an elevated position. (Compare Revelation 4:1.) Had John remained on earth in the vision, he would have been utterly perplexed by events on earth, but he was able to see those same events from heaven's perspective. Habakkuk soon realised that the apparent chaos and contradictions around him were all under divine control.

ii) "Make it plain upon tables." "Engrave it upon tablets" (JND). This reminds us, first of all, of the permanence of God's word. It is enduring in its importance. It also reminds us of the need to make the word of God plain to saint and sinner. We must not be enigmatic. The word of God is not just for private enjoyment: it is to be communicated. We must not, therefore, embellish or adorn it in any way.

iii) "That he may run that readeth it." The word of God is not sterile. It has not been given to us for academic discussion. It should have a practical effect on our lives. The study of prophecy should speed our feet, and give impetus to our lives. "Seeing then that all these things shall be dissolved, what manner of persons ought ye to be in all holy conversation and godliness ... Wherefore, beloved, seeing that ye look for such things, be diligent that ye may be found of him in peace, without spot, and blameless" (2 Pet. 3:11, 14).

b) The certainty of the answer, v.3

"The vision is yet for an appointed time, but at the end it shall speak, and not lie: though it tarry, wait for it; because it will surely come, it will not tarry." God is in control! He has a timetable! Everything will take place at "the appointed time". We can be sure that His timing is perfect. "As for God, his way is perfect" (Psalm 18:30). Whilst Habakkuk was not to expect the situation to be resolved immediately, he could be absolutely certain that God would bring everything to a satisfactory conclusion.

Notice other references to God's perfect timing. "But when the fulness of the time was come, God sent forth his Son" (Gal. 4:4); "For there is one God, and one mediator between God and men, the man Christ Jesus; who gave himself a ransom for all, to be testified in due time ('the testimony to be borne in its own times')" (1 Tim. 2:5-6); "Which in his times he shall shew, who is the blessed and only Potentate, the King of kings, and Lord of lords" (1 Tim. 6:15); "It is not for you to know the times or the seasons, which the Father hath put in his own power" (Acts 1:7). See also 1 Thessalonians 5 verse 1. We should notice:

i) God has a programme. Whilst world affairs seem to be totally out of control, God has an "appointed time". This necessitates taking a 'long view'. It is so easy to be immersed in the present, to be so bound up with ourselves and our circumstances, that we lose sight of God's ultimate purposes. See 1 Peter 1 verses 3-5 ("An inheritance ... reserved in heaven for you, who are kept by the power of God through faith unto salvation ready to be revealed in the last time"); 2 Corinthians 4 verse 17 ("For our light affliction, which is but for a moment, worketh for us a far more exceeding and eternal weight of glory"); Romans 8 verse 18 ("For I reckon that the sufferings of this present time are not worthy to be compared with the glory which shall be revealed in us").

ii) God's programme is certain. "At the end it shall speak, and not lie ... it will surely come." Paul reminds us that "whatsoever promises of God there are, in him is the yea, and in him the amen, for glory to God by us" (2 Cor. 1:20, JND). There may be an interval before it is fulfilled, but its fulfilment is certain.

iii) God's programme requires patience. "Though it tarry, wait for it." The passage is cited in Hebrews 10 verses 35-37. Note the context: "But call to remembrance the former days, in which, after ye were illuminated, ye endured a great fight of afflictions" (v.32). But persecution had brought the danger of reverting to Judaism. Hence, "Cast not away therefore your confidence, which hath great recompence of reward. For ye have need of patience (Habakkuk, "wait for it"), that, after ye have done the will of God, ye might receive the promise (as in Habakkuk). For yet a little while, and he that shall come will come, and will not tarry". There is a point to patience! We "shew the Lord's death ***till*** he come" (1 Cor. 11:26). We wait ***"until*** the day break, and the shadows flee away" (Song of Solomon 2:17). We must "let patience have her perfect work, that ye may be perfect and entire, wanting nothing" (James 1:4).

O blessed hope, with this elate,
Let not our hearts be desolate,
But strong in faith, in patience wait
Until He come.

Notice that in Habakkuk, it is, "***It*** will surely come, ***it*** will not tarry". In Hebrews, it is, ***"He*** that shall come will come, and will not tarry". The New Testament interprets the Old Testament in terms of the Lord's return. We must ***"Wait for it!"***

iv) God's programme will not be delayed. "It will not tarry." This does not mean that the fulfilment of the vision was imminent, but that nothing could delay the programme when the time comes for its implementation.

c) The content of the answer, vv.4-20

As we have noticed, Habakkuk is told to "write the vision" (v.2), and that "the vision is yet for an appointed time" (v.3). The vision itself is now disclosed to Habakkuk. God answers the protest and perplexity of His servant by enabling him to see two things: ***(i)*** God's judgment of the wicked, and ***(ii)*** God's glory in the world.

In connection with the first, we must notice, amongst other things, the fivefold use of "Woe" (vv.6, 9, 12, 15, 19). In connection with the second, we must notice that "the earth shall be filled with the knowledge of the glory of the LORD, as the waters cover the sea" (v.14). This passage emphasises two important matters: the pathway of the righteous (v.4) and the punishment of the unrighteous (vv.5-20).

i) The pathway of the righteous, v.4

As we will see in greater detail, God will judge the wicked in the world, and He will display His glory in the world. But how are God's people to conduct themselves as they wait for this to take place? We have already seen that they are to wait with patience: "Though it tarry, wait for it; because it will surely come, it will not tarry" (v.3). We now learn that they were to wait in faith. "The just shall live by faith." This is emphasised by means of a comparison: "Behold, his soul which is lifted up is not upright in him: but the just shall live by his faith." Notice therefore:

- ***Those that are "not upright".*** They are marked by self-confidence and pride. They are ***"lifted up"***. Undoubtedly, in the first instance, this refers to the Chaldeans who had made a god of their own power. See Chapter 1 verse 11 (JND): "This his power is become his god', and RV, "Whose might is his god". Nebuchadnezzar exemplifies this: "Is not this great Babylon, that I have built for the house of the kingdom by the might of my power, and for the honour of my majesty?" (Dan. 4:30).

- ***Those who are described as "the just".*** They are marked by "faith". "But ***the just shall live by his faith***." That is, by resting on what God has said. Note that the word "faith" only occurs twice in the AV Old Testament: here and in Deuteronomy 32 verse 20. But it translates a Hebrew word occurring some fifty times in the Old Testament. Its first occurrence is in Exodus 17 verse 12, "Moses' hands were ***steady*** ..." See also Lamentations 3 verse 23, "Great is thy ***faithfulness***". It emphasises the link between behaviour (faithfulness) and belief (faith). This is the secret of an upright life in the circumstances described in Chapter 1 verses 2-4. It is the faith of a lifetime, rather than the faith of a moment. This is also cited in Hebrews 10 verses 37-38, "For yet a little while, and he that shall come will come, and will not tarry. ***Now the just shall live by faith***". So it is a case of continuing in faith, waiting for the coming of the Lord and for future glory, although subject to perplexity and pressure. This is how men like Daniel and Ezekiel lived in the midst of Babylonian supremacy, when all seemed lost. They lived in view of the promises of God.

We should note the different emphasis in each of the three New Testament citations of Habakkuk 2 verse 14:

- ***Romans 1:17***, "For therein is the righteousness of God revealed from faith to faith: as it is written, The ***just*** shall live by faith". It has been nicely said that Habakkuk is 'the great-grandfather of the Reformation'.

- *Galatians 3:11*, "But that no man is justified by the law in the sight of God, it is evident: for, The just shall live by ***faith***". That is, by faith, as opposed to works.

- *Hebrews 10:38-39*, "Now the just shall ***live*** by faith: but if any man draw back, my soul shall have no pleasure in him. But we are not of them who draw back unto perdition; but of them that believe to the saving of the soul". The Old Testament saints lived by faith.

ii) The punishment of the unrighteous, vv.5-20

It is significant that the Chaldeans are not mentioned by name. This does not mean, of course, that they are excluded from the passage, but by omitting direct reference to them, God sets out the reasons for judgment on ***all*** wicked nations. We must notice, however, that the judgment of the Chaldeans, and of all wicked nations, is not God's ***ultimate*** purpose. Having brought the nations of the world to nothing (v.13), He will then fill the world with His glory (v.14). The reasons for judgment are set out in the passage.

- *Sinful acquisition, vv.5-8. "Woe* to him that increaseth that which is not his!" (v.6). "Yea also, because he transgresseth by wine, he is a proud man, neither keepeth at home, who enlargeth his desire as hell, and is as death, and cannot be satisfied, but gathereth unto him all nations, and heapeth unto him all people (plural: 'peoples', JND)."

The expression, "he transgresseth by wine" ('the wine is treacherous', JND), evidently refers, not to literal wine (although that can be 'treacherous': remember Noah, and Belshazzar), but to the heady wine of success. "Intoxicated by ambitious conquest, he roams the earth to enlarge the borders of his realm" (M. C. Unger). The expression, "neither keepeth at home", emphasises the desire for territorial expansion. The Chaldeans wanted world domination: "all nations ... all people" (v.5). This is a warning to ***us*** against covetousness, and prosperity through greed. The Chaldeans were intent on theft and plunder. The believer is to display the reverse. "Let him that stole steal no more: but rather let him labour, working with his hands the thing which is good, that he may have to ***give*** to him that needeth" (Eph.

4:28). In a society marked by consumerism and materialism, ***"the just shall live by faith"***.

The principle of sowing and reaping, found everywhere in Scripture, is applicable here. See verses 6-8: the very oppressed peoples would "take up a parable against him, and a taunting proverb ('riddle', JND) against him, and say, Woe to him that increaseth that which is not his! How long? And to him that ladeth himself with thick clay!" The words, "that ladeth himself with thick clay", evidently mean, 'ladeth himself with pledges', that is, pledges of tribute money which would have been written on clay tablets. The Chaldeans crushed weaker nations in order to secure financial gain, but they would reap where they had sown: "Shall they not rise up suddenly that shall bite thee, and awake that shall vex thee, and thou shalt be for booties unto them? Because thou hast ***spoiled*** many nations, all the remnant of the people shall ***spoil*** thee; because of men's blood, and for the violence of the land, of the city, and of all that dwell therein". See also verse 10. So God ***will*** do right by His holy character! Habakkuk's statement was absolutely correct. See Chapter 1 verse 13. Compare divine judgment on Edom (Obadiah) and Nineveh (Nahum).

- Selfish ambition, vv.9-11. "***Woe*** to him that coveteth an evil covetousness to his house, that he may set his nest on high, that he may be delivered from the power of evil!" In a word, security! This spotlights pride of dynasty. Empire building! The continuance of name and position. The word "house" is not used in a literal sense, but metaphorically for family. The New Testament warns us against love of position. Diotrephes was censured for this very reason: "I wrote unto the church: but Diotrephes, who loveth to have the pre-eminence among them, receiveth us not" (3 John 9). The apostle Paul had no such ambitions: "Not for that we have dominion over your faith, but are helpers of your joy: for by faith ye stand" (2 Cor. 1:24). We should also remember that security is the obsession of our age. People will do almost anything to achieve material security! ***But "the just shall live by faith".***

Notice, again, the law of sowing and reaping: "Thou hast consulted shame to thy house by cutting off many people, and hast sinned against thy soul. For the stone shall cry out of the wall, and the beam out of the timber shall answer it" (vv.10-11). Once again, the language is used metaphorically: the very people and materials used by the Chaldeans to build their interests would cry out for judgment on them.

- ***Sinful glory, vv.12-14.*** *"**Woe*** to him that buildeth a town with blood, and stablisheth a city by iniquity!" The Babylonians built gilded cities, imposing temples, and grand monuments, but they did it with slave labour! It was all for their own glory. Man's glory began with Babel: "Go to, let ***us*** build ***us*** a city and a tower, whose top may reach unto heaven; and let ***us*** make ***us*** a name" (Gen. 11:4). It was enshrined in Nebuchadnezzar, of whom God said, "Thou art this head of gold", and he promptly made an image, evidently of himself, completely of gold! Man's glory will end with the destruction of latter Babylon. See Revelation 18.

But what will be the result of such self glory? See verse 13, "Behold, is it not of the LORD of hosts that the people shall labour in the very fire, and the people shall weary themselves for very vanity?" or, 'Behold, is it not of Jehovah of hosts that the peoples labour for the fire, and the nations weary themselves in vain?' (JND). Whilst similar language is used of Babylon (see Jeremiah 51:58), the wording here ('peoples ... nations') goes beyond one particular nation. So, it is of God that nations come to power, only ultimately to be humbled and destroyed. Their greed and ambition is nothing else but 'labour for the fire', or destruction. Nations will fall in spite of their towering success and immense power. See, for example, the collapse of the USSR. (These notes were written in 2004. At the moment, Vladimir Putin is attempting to restore the USSR.)

In this way, God, who controls history, whether past, present or future, clears the ground for the display of ***His*** glory in the world. "For the earth shall be filled (not with oppression and injustice) with the knowledge of the glory of the LORD, as the waters cover the sea." (Compare Isaiah 11:9.) This passage, therefore, looks forward to the time when the greatest of all human kingdoms - the kingdom of the Beast, with all its power and wisdom - will be destroyed, and the millennial kingdom of Christ is established. See, for example, Isaiah 11 & 12. This is "the vision" to which verses 2-3 refer. We look beyond the fading glory of this world, to the time when "the earth shall be filled with the knowledge of the glory of the LORD as the waters cover the sea". The glory of the Lord will be like the sea: it will cause awe and wonder. Its tremendous power and limitless expanse make it a picture of God's glory which will fill the earth in the same way that the sea covers its bed. The depth of the sea reminds us that there will be nothing superficial about the glory of God! With this in mind, ***"the just shall live by faith"***.

- ***Shameful humiliation, vv.15-17.*** *"**Woe*** unto him that giveth his neighbour drink, that puttest thy bottle to him, and makest him drunken also, that thou mayest look on their nakedness!" Once again, in the context of the passage, the reference is not so much to literal intoxication, but to the cunning subtlety of nations seeking to undermine other nations. Beguiling other nations to their fate. On the other hand, the language could depict weaker nations reeling under the power of stronger nations. See, for example, Revelation 14 verse 8, "She (Babylon) made all nations drink of the wine of the wrath of her fornication". But in it all, ***"the just shall live by faith"***.

In connection with "the violence of Lebanon", M. C. Unger observes: "The Chaldean, like the successive monarchs of several nations, had cut down the timbers of Lebanon, hunted its wild beasts, and decimated its cattle. His violent and shameful misuse of God's creation - both animate and inanimate - as well as his abuse of the Lord's own people in Judaea, were potent causes of the Chaldean's downfall, and the vindication of the Lord's infinitely holy nature". A case of biblical ecology!

- Senseless idolatry, vv.18-20. "Woe unto him that saith to the wood, Awake; to the dumb stone, Arise, it shall teach!" Idols are ***manufactured:*** "the maker thereof hath graven it ... the maker of his work trusteth therein" (v.18). Idols are ***misleading***: the "molten image" is "a teacher of lies" (v.18). Idols are ***mute:*** "dumb idols ... dumb stone" (vv.18-19). These verses stress the folly of worshipping the labour of human hands! (Like cars, homes etc.) They are impressive, but lifeless. No wonder John concludes his First Epistle with, "Little children, keep yourselves from idols" (1 John 5:21). But ***"the just shall live by faith"***.

After all the activity and noise described in these verses, a voice is heard: "Keep silence". Here is the complete quotation: "But the LORD is in his holy temple (compare Psalm 11:4): let all the earth keep silence before him" (v.20). If there is anything to say, it must be in the language of Romans 11 verses 33-36. Those that worship the "dumb stone" will be dumb themselves. ***Who is the Speaker?*** He is "the LORD (Jehovah)"; ***Where is He?*** He is "in his holy temple"; ***What should men do?*** "Keep silence before him."

Here is the definitive answer to Habakkuk's protest and perplexity. God had not abdicated His government. He "is in his holy temple". Everything is completely under his control. Nothing has changed in two thousand six hundred years. God has not abdicated His government. He is still in absolute control of world affairs.

Faith looks beyond the circumstances, and sees a throne – just like Isaiah: "I saw also the Lord sitting upon a throne, high and lifted up, and his train filled the temple" (Isa. 6:1), and just like Micaiah: "I saw the LORD sitting upon his throne, and all the host of heaven standing on his right hand and on his left" (2 Chron. 18:18).

Now what will Habakkuk say?

HABAKKUK

4) Chapter 3:1-19

As we have noticed, the prophecy of Habakkuk, which is a dialogue between the prophet and God, can be divided into five sections:

1) Habakkuk's problem, 1:1-4
2) God's answer, 1:5-11
3) Habakkuk's protest, 1:12 - 2:1
4) God's answer, 2:2-20
5) Habakkuk's praise, 3:1-19

The prophet has now seen that God always acts in complete consistency with His own character: ***(i)*** In dealing with evil in His own people, and ***(ii)*** In dealing with evil in the nations. In both cases, He is preparing for the day when His purpose for mankind will be fulfilled, and "the earth shall be filled with the knowledge of the glory (not of the Chaldean or any other nation) of the LORD" (2:14). So God's purposes are to be understood with reference to long term, not short term, considerations. As we shall see, Habakkuk no longer questions God's ways: he takes the place of humility: "I ... was afraid" (v.2). He no longer complains: he takes the place of an intercessor: "O Lord, revive thy work in the midst of the years" (v.2). In the meantime, "the just shall live by his faith" (2:4).

Having seen that God will bring everything to a satisfactory conclusion, and fill the earth with His glory, Habakkuk utters his sublime prayer. The chapter may be divided as follows: ***(1)*** His prayer (vv.1-2); ***(2)*** His vision (vv.3-15); ***(3)*** His faith (vv.16-19).

1) THE PRAYER OF HABAKKUK, vv.1-2

Chapter 2 concludes with silence on earth: "The LORD is in his holy temple:

let all the earth keep silence before him" (v.20). Chapter 3 commences and concludes with praise. We must notice:

a) The word of God promoted praise

"A prayer of Habakkuk the prophet upon Shigionoth. O LORD, I have heard thy speech, and was afraid" (vv.1-2). So we have a psalm from a prophet! For Shigionoth, see Psalm 7 with its superscript, "Shiggaion of David, which he sang unto the LORD, concerning the words of Cush the Benjamite". We are told that the words Shigionoth (plural) and Shiggaion (singular) refer to a military composition. They probably indicate the rhythm. But although the precise meaning of the two words is not easily determined, they do indicate that the compositions were to be set to music. This is clear from the concluding words of the prophecy: "To the chief singer (JND, 'musician') on my stringed instruments" (v.19).

So Habakkuk heard the word of God ("O LORD, I have heard thy speech", v.1), and responded in praise to God. This is fitting in view of the fact that God had ended His answer to Habakkuk's protest with reference to His majesty and omnipotence: "The LORD is in his holy temple" (2:20). How much are ***we*** affected by the ways and purposes of God? We should be a praising people as well!

b) The word of God promoted godly fear

"O LORD, I have heard thy speech, and was afraid" (v.2). Of what was Habakkuk afraid? Certainly not of the future. God had dealt with that problem. He was afraid of God Himself, possibly because he had dared to question the ways of God. However, Habakkuk did exhibit "the fear of the LORD", reminding us of Isaiah 66 verse 2: "To this man will I look, even to him that is poor and of a contrite spirit, and trembleth at my word". There is nothing inconsistent between praise and godly fear. The word of God should produce in us "reverence and godly fear" (Heb. 12:28).

c) The word of God promoted intercession

"O LORD, revive thy work in the midst of the years, in the midst of the years make known; in wrath remember mercy" (v.2). According to Gesenius *(Hebrew-Chaldea Lexicon to the Old Testament),* the word "revive" means, 'to cause to live', in the sense of 'accomplish'. According to D. Martyn Lloyd-

Jones *(From Fear to Faith)*, the Hebrew word has the primary meaning of 'preserve' or 'keep alive'. Habakkuk had demanded justice (1:2-4), but now he says, "Remember mercy!" He refers here to God's covenant with Israel. Habakkuk did not ask God to change His mind, and deliver Judah from the Chaldeans. He had now seen that they were an integral part of God's purpose for His people, that is, in chastening them. But he does ask that God will work out His covenant-purposes for them, and this must involve the preservation of a remnant. This is ***praying within the will of God***. His prayer was partially answered in Ezra 9 verse 8 when there was "a little reviving in our bondage". Note particularly the words, "In the midst of the years". That is, in the present circumstances. Not, 'at the end of the years'. Habakkuk addressed the present in the light of the future. The burden of his prayer is 'act now!', even though it is 'not yet!' (2:3). He knew that the time had not fully come, but asks the Lord to act in the meantime.

So Habakkuk intercedes: ***(i)*** that God will work out His purposes, and ***(ii)*** that God, because He is God, would act according to His nature: in wrath, and yet, in mercy. And so He did. Even when Judah was under the sentence of divine wrath in Babylon, He showed mercy. We may therefore notice that Habakkuk's prayer includes, ***reverence*** for God, ***revival*** of the work, and ***remembrance*** of mercy.

2) THE VISION OF HABAKKUK, vv.3-15

Habakkuk received this vision in answer to his request, "O LORD, revive thy work in the midst of the years, in the midst of the years make known; in wrath remember mercy" (v.2). While, as we have noted, God partially answered the request of His servant in the return from exile, the words, "in wrath remember mercy", have a strong prophetic connotation. His prayer would be fully answered at the end-time.

God answered Habakkuk's prayer with this tremendous vision. It is couched in language strikingly reminiscent of the exodus from Egypt, and the conquest of Canaan, and this is summed up in the words: "Thou wentest forth for the salvation of thy people" (v.13). In this connection, we should notice the following: ***(i)*** verses 3-8 recall Israel's deliverance from Egypt; ***(ii)*** verses 9-10 recall events in the wilderness journey; ***(iii)*** verses 11-14 recall events in the conquest of Canaan. But some details have to be forced to fit this interpretation, and it is better to take the vision as future, when God, in His wrath at the end-time, will remember mercy, and intervene to save His people. But if the vision does refer to the end-time, why make clear references to the exodus and following events? It is, surely, to assure Habakkuk that God is quite capable of intervening on behalf of His people. He had done it once, and will do so again. He will, indeed, 'revive his work'! Habakkuk is taken beyond the coming of the Chaldeans, to the coming of the Lord! We must notice the active verbs: "came" (v.3), "stood ... measured ... beheld … drove asunder" (v.6), "ride" (v.8), "cleave" (v.9), "march" (v.12), "wentest forth" (v.13), "walk" (v.15). God in action!

We must note the following:

a) The direction from which He comes, v.3

"God (Eloah: singular of Elohim: 'the Adorable One') came (the tense is 'cometh') from Teman, and the Holy One from mount Paran." That is, He comes from the south. Teman and Paran are on opposite sides of the deep rift valley known as the Arabah. Teman is in Edomite territory. Compare Isaiah 63 verses 1-4, "Who is this that cometh from Edom with dyed garments from Bozrah? this that is glorious in his apparel, travelling in the greatness of his strength? I that speak in righteousness, mighty to save. Wherefore art thou red in thine apparel, and thy garments like him that treadeth in the winefat. I have trodden the winepress alone ... for the day of vengeance is in mine heart, and the year of my redeemed is come".

What is He doing in the south? Possibly, having come to the mount of Olives, and opened the escape route from the besieged city (Zech. 14:2), He will go south to deal with the enemy there, and this passage describes His return to Jerusalem. It should be noted, however, that this is the area in which Sinai is located: "The LORD came from Sinai, and rose from Seir unto them; he shined forth from mount Paran, and he came with ten thousands of saints: from his right hand went a fiery law for them" (Deut. 33:2). He comes, therefore, from the area in which the covenant was made.

b) The description of His glory, vv.3-5

"His glory covered the heavens, and the earth was full of his praise" (v.3). This should be compared with Revelation 5 verse 13, "And every creature which is in heaven, and on the earth … heard I saying, Blessing, and honour, and glory, and power, be unto him that sitteth upon the throne, and unto the Lamb for ever and ever". We must notice:

i) "His brightness was as the light" (v.4). Compare 1 Timothy 6 verse 16, "Who only hath immortality, dwelling in the light which no man can approach unto" and 1 John 1 verse 5. "God is light, and in him is no darkness at all".

ii) "He had horns coming out of his hand" (v.4). Horns are a scriptural emblem for strength, and this could therefore convey the strength of His work. But although the word is quite literally 'horns', it seems more likely that this refers to rays of light. "Rays [came forth] from his hand" (JND).

iii) "There was the hiding of his power" (v.4). That is, even with this revelation, His essential glory was covered. "Thou canst not see my face, for there shall no man see me, and live" (Exodus 33:20); "Whom no man hath seen, nor can see" (1 Tim. 6:16). The things that Habakkuk saw were not the revelation of God's power, but the "hiding of his power"!

iv) "Before him went the pestilence, and burning coals went forth at his feet" (v.5). This is reminiscent of the plagues in Egypt. The "burning coals" might refer to the plague of hail, which was more than 'white lumps'! "Hail, and fire mingled with the hail." See also Revelation 16 verse 21.

c) The deliberation in His coming, vv.6-7

"He stood, and measured the earth: he beheld, and drove asunder the nations." Nothing will be done in the heat of the moment. There will be no hasty decisions. He assessed the situation, and then acted. This must include His assessment of man's wickedness. No power is too great to withstand Him: "He … measured the earth." No political power is too great to withstand Him: "He … drove asunder the nations". Notice the effect on ***(i)*** geography, and ***(ii)*** on men:

- ***On geography, v.6.*** "The everlasting mountains were scattered", literally 'shattered'. "The perpetual hills did bow." There is no reason why this should not be understood quite literally. See, for example, the division and movement of the mount of Olives (Zech. 14:4). Note the comment: "His ways are everlasting". God will repeat His past dealings when acting for the deliverance of His people.

- ***On men, v.7.*** This refers particularly to the nomadic tribes: "I saw the tents of Cushan in affliction: and the curtains of the land of Midian did tremble". These people were accustomed to flapping tent curtains, but now they are utterly terrified!

d) The desire for His people, vv.8-9

The questions here are asked, but not answered. "Was the LORD displeased against the rivers? was thine (notice the change here; he had been speaking ***about*** God: now he speaks ***to*** God) anger against the rivers? was thy wrath against the sea, that thou didst ride upon thine horses and thy chariots of salvation?" (v.8). In the words of M. C. Unger: 'It was not the Lord's displeasure against the waters of the Red Sea, but His delight in intervening on behalf of His people's "salvation" (v.13)'. But while, as Unger suggests, this alludes to the passage of the Red Sea, we must remember that God will do the same in the future. See Isaiah 11 verse 15. Habakkuk refers here to events at the end-time. The statement, "Thou didst cleave the earth with rivers", also points to the future, rather than the past. See Zechariah 14 verse 8. But see Psalm 105 verse 41 and Psalm 114 verse 8.

The words, "Thy bow was made quite naked, according to the oaths of the tribes, even thy word. Selah" (v.9), have given translators some headaches! RV/ASV are identical: "Thy bow was made quite bare, the oaths to the tribes were a sure word". JND is rather complicated! ("Thy bow was made quite naked, the rods of discipline sworn according to thy word.") It seems, therefore, that in His desire for the blessing of His people, God will intervene to ensure the safe passage of His people as they return to the land (v.8), and fulfil every promise made to them (v.9).

e) The deference of creation, vv.10-11

All creation bows to the voice of the Creator as He comes: ***(i)*** The mountains (v.10): "The mountains saw thee, and they trembled"; ***(ii)*** The waters (v.10): "the overflowing of the water passed by: the deep uttered his voice, and lifted up his hands on high" (Compare Joshua 3:16); ***(iii)*** The sun and moon (v.11): "The sun and the moon stood still in their habitation". The allusion to past events is clear: see Joshua 10 verses 12-13, "And the sun stood still, and the moon stayed". But this will evidently be repeated in the future. See Zechariah 14 verses 6-7; Psalm 114 verses 3-7.

The words, "At the light of thine arrows they went ('At the light of thine arrows which shot forth' JND), and at the shining of thy glittering spear" (v.11), could refer to lightning and hailstones respectively. For the former, see Psalm 18 verse 14, "Yea, he sent out his arrows, and scattered them;

and he shot out lightnings and discomfited them". For the latter, see Joshua 10 verse 11 and Psalm 18 verse 13. But it seems more likely to understand this with reference to God's power. Nothing can impede His coming. At the assertion of His mighty power of conquest ("arrows" and "spear"), even creation must bow!

f) The defeat of His enemies, vv.12-15

"***Thou*** didst march through the land in indignation, ***thou*** didst thresh the heathen in anger. ***Thou*** wentest forth for the salvation of thy people, even for salvation with thine anointed; ***thou*** woundedst the head out of the house of the wicked ... ***Thou*** didst strike through with his staves the head of his villages ... ***Thou*** didst walk through the sea with thine horses, through the heap of great waters." It is the march of a Conqueror!

Notice the references to "salvation". The ***source*** of salvation: "thy ***chariots*** of salvation" (v.8); the ***subjects*** of salvation: "the salvation of thy people" (v.13); the ***song*** of salvation: "I will joy in the God of my salvation" (v.18).

Although the word "anointed" (v.13) is singular, it evidently refers to Israel. See JND: "Thou wentest forth for the salvation of thy people, for the salvation of thine anointed". Compare Psalm 105 verses 14-15, "He suffered no man to do them wrong: yea, he reproved kings for their sakes, saying, Touch not mine anointed".

But salvation from whom? "Thou woundedst the head out of the house of ***the wicked,*** by discovering the foundation unto the neck. Selah" (v.13), or "Thou didst smite off the head from the house of the wicked ..." (JND). "Thou didst strike through with his staves the head of his villages" (v.14) or "Thou didst strike through with his own spears the head of his leaders" (JND). Compare Psalm 110 verse 6, "He shall wound the heads (literally, 'head': singular) over many countries". These verses therefore describe the salvation of His people from the power of a great enemy. There can be little doubt that this is an allusion to "the beast". No power or obstacle will be able to prevent total victory. Once again, the language recalls deliverance from the power of Pharaoh (perhaps from the power of the kings of Canaan: see Joshua 10/11): "They came out as a whirlwind to scatter me: their rejoicing was to devour the poor secretly. Thou didst walk through the sea with thine horses, through the heap of great waters" (vv.14-15). Past deliverance will be repeated.

3) THE FAITH OF HABAKKUK, vv.16-19

We must notice here: ***(a)*** His reaction (v.16); ***(b)*** His resolve (vv.17-18); ***(c)*** His rejoicing (vv.18-19).

a) His reaction, v.16

"When I heard, my belly trembled; my lips quivered at the voice: rottenness entered into my bones, and I trembled in myself." Like Isaiah, Habakkuk cried in effect, "Woe is me!" The vision of God's majesty and power caused the end of all argument. But the same vision, which caused Habakkuk so much fear, brought "rest in the day of trouble" or "that I might rest in the day of distress (like Noah, meaning 'rest'), when their invader shall come up against the people" (JND).

So the vision caused Habakkuk personal distress. Who or what was he in the light of it? Totally unworthy! It also brought him rest: God had everything under control! His terror is turned into trust. It is summed up in 2 Corinthians 12 verse 10, "When I am weak, then am I strong".

b) His resolve, vv.17-18

Because Habakkuk had seen the purpose of God and the power of God, he could rejoice in the most appalling circumstances, for "the just shall live by his faith" (2:4). "Although the fig tree shall not blossom, neither shall fruit be in the vines; the labour of the olive shall fail, and the fields shall yield no meat: the flock shall be cut off from the fold, and there shall be no herd in the stalls (and that was what was going to happen), yet I will rejoice in the LORD, I will joy in the God of my salvation." What sublime faith! These words refer to the 'scorched earth' policy of the Chaldeans. There is nothing left but God! Habakkuk knew that "a man's life consisteth not in the abundance of the things which he possesseth" (Luke 12:15).

c) His rejoicing, vv.18-19

Notice that Habakkuk rejoices in a personal relationship with God in an uncertain world. "Yet ***I*** will rejoice in the LORD, ***I*** will joy in the God of ***my*** salvation. The LORD God is ***my*** strength, and he will make ***my*** feet like hinds' feet, and he will make ***me*** to walk upon ***my*** high places."

- He is rejoicing in adverse circumstances. We can easily rejoice in favourable circumstances. Habakkuk had been through a bruising experience. Paul could say, "I have learned, in whatsoever state I am ... to be content" (Phil. 4:11-12). Job could say, "Though he slay me, yet will I trust in him" (Job 13:15). Jeremiah could say, "It is of the LORD's mercies that we are not consumed, because his compassions fail not. They are new every morning: great is thy faithfulness" (Lam. 3:22-23).

- He is not rejoicing because of his circumstances. He is rejoicing "In the God of my salvation".

- He was rejoicing because something infinitely better lay ahead! He looked beyond the immediate to the ultimate. The coming desolation of Judah was but an integral part of God's purpose. He rises above his frustration and misunderstanding of Chapter 1. His complaint turns to rejoicing! Before, Habakkuk was uncertain and unsure, but he had learnt that he can trust God in the enigmas of life. He is content at the end, although he has nothing - apart from joy in God! When Paul was in prison with nothing but the clothes in which he stood, he was able to say, "I have all, and abound" (Phil. 4:18). He had nothing, but he had everything! In the world, joy co-exists with success. But here we have impoverishment. In the world, joy co-exists with prosperity. But here we have poverty. In the world, joy co-exists with acclaim. But here we have persecution.

Men in Habakkuk's position would doubt the future: but he rejoices in the Lord! Men without Christ would ***doubt,*** but ***we*** can "rejoice in hope of the glory of God" (Rom. 5:2). Men without Christ would ***despair.*** They can go through suffering with tenacity, fortitude, stoicism, but not with joy! ***We*** "rejoice in our tribulations" (Rom. 5:3, ASV). Men without Christ would ***dread.*** But ***we*** can "joy in God" (Rom. 5:11). We too can say "I will rejoice in the LORD, I will joy in the God of my salvation". The man who began with bewilderment and uncertainty, ends by treading his high places with sure feet far above the mists and darkness of earth. He is overwhelmed in Chapter 1, where he walks by sight. But he rides above it all in Chapter 3, where he walks by faith! "To walk upon my high places" describes balance and sure-footedness with a steep precipice on either side.

So Habakkuk concludes with ***salvation*** ("the God of my salvation"), ***strength*** ("the LORD God is my strength": he did not find his strength in logical argument or enlightenment), and ***stability*** ("he will make my feet like hinds' feet"). Habakkuk realised that in the deprivation resulting from the coming Babylonian invasion, God was working out His purpose and would achieve the ultimate blessing of His people.

OTHER TITLES AVAILABLE IN THE SERIES:

Joshua, Judges, Ruth	9781910513439
1 Samuel	9781907731716
2 Samuel	9781907731921
Ezra, Nehemiah, Esther	9781910513095
Ezekiel	9781914273155
Hosea, Joel, Amos, Obadiah	9781910513781
Matthew	9781910513934
Luke	9781909803541
The Acts of the Apostles	9781907731457
1 Corinthians	9781912522422
2 Corinthians	9781912522644
Philippians, Colossians, 1 & 2 Thessalonians	9781910513224
Galatians, Ephesians	9781912522897
1 & 2 Timothy, Titus, Philemon	9781910513552
Revelation	9781914273315